Reading the Fifty States

Booktalks, Response Activities, and More

Nancy Polette

LIBRARIES

U N L I M I T E D

A Member of the Greenwood Publishing Group

Westport, Connecticut • London

Library of Congress Cataloging-in-Publication Data

Polette, Nancy.
  Reading the fifty states : booktalks, response activities, and more / Nancy Polette.
     p. cm.
  Includes bibliographical references and index.
  ISBN 978-1-59158-820-7 (alk. paper)
  1. Social sciences—Study and teaching (Elementary)—United States. 2. Activity programs in education—United States. 3. Reading promotion—United States. I. Title.
  LB1584.P65   2009
  372.83'044—dc22   2008038286

British Library Cataloguing in Publication Data is available.

Library of Congress Catalog Card Number: 2008038286
ISBN: 978-1-59158-820-7

First published in 2009

Libraries Unlimited, 88 Post Road West, Westport, CT 06881
A Member of the Greenwood Publishing Group, Inc.
www.lu.com

Printed in the United States of America

The paper used in this book complies with the
Permanent Paper Standard issued by the National
Information Standards Organization (Z39.48–1984).

10   9   8   7   6   5   4   3   2   1

Contents

Part One
The Fifty States

Part Two
Reader Response Activities

Introduction

Traditionally, instruction in the social studies area has been *content* rather than *process* oriented. In many classrooms students are expected to acquire a certain body of knowledge by relying heavily on the cognitive areas of memory and comprehension, with little attention given to higher-level thinking or the affective domain. For example:

Low-level thinking processes: Name the capital city and major products of each state.

Higher-level thinking processes: If you could relocate your state capital, where would you move it? Defend your choice of site.

In both examples the student is working with content. However, in the higher-level example he or she is not only gaining content knowledge, but is also learning to analyze and to critically evaluate. Both higher-level thinking processes are important, and the thinking skills acquired can be transferred to other subject areas.

Learning state capitals will not help the student understand how the environment of each state affects the people who live there. Nor will the student become aware of how the cultures brought by early settlers still influence the lives of the citizens today. What better way to truly discover the history and culture of each of the fifty states than by exploring novels set in each of the states?

Reading the Fifty States offers four booktalks for each state and twenty response and research activities to choose from. All activities call for higher-level thinking, and most allow the student to respond in creative ways. In addition, the student response activities in the second part of the book are based on national standards in language arts and social studies.

Reading the Fifty States will allow students and teachers alike to add a whole new dimension to the social studies program by emphasizing history and geography through the people who lived it.

Activities are based on selected national standards in language arts and social studies:

1. Recognize and investigate problems, formulate and propose solutions supported by reason and evidence.

2. Express and interpret information and ideas.

3. Learn and contribute productively as individuals and as members of groups.

4. Recognize and apply connections of important information and ideas within and among learning areas.

5. Acquire, analyze, interpret, and communicate information or data by observing and recognizing changes over time. Sequence, order, and classify information.

6. Form definitions based on observations and infer, generalize, and predict outcomes.

7. Identify a problem, formulate and evaluate alternative solutions.

8. Draw conclusions about processes or outcomes and relate or apply knowledge gained.

9. Apply word analysis and vocabulary skills to comprehend selections.

10. Apply reading strategies to improve understanding and fluency.

11. Comprehend a broad range of reading materials.

12. Understand how literary elements are used to convey meaning.

13. Read and interpret a variety of literary works.

14. Use correct grammar, spelling, punctuation, capitalization, and structure.

15. Compose well-organized and coherent writing for specific purposes and audiences.

16. Communicate ideas in writing to accomplish a variety of purposes.

17. Listen effectively in formal and informal situations.

18. Speak effectively, using language appropriate to the situation and audience.

19. Locate, organize, and use information from a variety of sources to answer questions, solve problems, and communicate ideas.

20. Analyze and evaluate information from a variety of sources.

21. Apply acquired information, concepts, and ideas to communicate in a variety of formats.

Compiling a State Notebook

1. Choose a state. After reading the booktalks for novels set in that state, locate and read one of the novels.

2. Write a one-page summary of the novel. Include author, title, publisher, and copyright date. Be sure to include descriptions of the characters, the central problem of the novel, and the solution.

3. In one-half to one page, describe the setting of the novel. What aspects of the setting reveal information about the state?

4. Watch newspapers for articles about events that happen in the state. Collect and arrange articles chronologically in your notebook.

5. Watch newspapers for articles about well-known people from the state. Clip the articles and add them to your notebook.

6. Choose four or more of the research activities from the second part of this book. Complete the activities and add them to your notebook.

7. Compile a bibliography of other novels whose setting is the state you have chosen. Include author, title, publisher, date, and a one-sentence description.

    Example: MISSISSIPPI

Taylor, Mildred. *The Friendship*. Dial Books, 1987.
    Four children witness a confrontation between an elderly black man and a white storekeeper in rural Mississippi in the 1930s.

Series and Titles about the Fifty States

Series (include individual titles for each state)

Discover America State by State. Sleeping Bear Press.

From Sea to Shining Sea. Children's Press.

Hello. U.S.A. Lerner Publications.

Portraits of the States. Gareth Stevens.

Rookie Read About Geography. Children's Press.

World Almanac Library of States. World Almanac Publications.

Individual Titles

Cheney, Lynne. *Our 50 States: A Family Adventure Across America.* Simon & Schuster, 2006.

D'Amico, Joan. *The United States Cookbook: Fabulous Foods and Fascinating Facts from All 50 States.* John Wiley, 2000.

Davis, Kenneth. *Don't Know Much About the Fifty States.* HarperCollins, 2006.

Davis, Todd. *The New Big Book of America.* Courage Books, 2002.

Krull, Kathleen. *Wish You Were Here: Emily's Guide to the Fifty States.* Doubleday, 1997.

Leedy, Loreen. *Celebrate the 50 States.* Holiday House, 1999.

Miller, Millie. *The United States of America: A State by State Guide.* Scholastic, 1999.

National Geographic Book Service. *Picture Atlas of Our Fifty States.* National Geographic, 1978.

Ross, Frank. *Stories of the States.* Crowell, 1969.

Travis, George. *State Facts.* Rourke Press, 1999.

Yaccarino, Don. *Go, Go, America: Fifty States of Fun.* Scholastic, 2008.

Periodical

Crinkles. Libraries Unlimited. Features a state three to four times a year.

Part One

The Fifty States

Alabama Fact Sheet

Capital: Montgomery

Largest City: Birmingham

Entered the Union: December 14, 1819

Tree: Southern longleaf pine

Flower: Camelia

Bird: Yellowhammer

Rivers: Tombigbee, Alabama, Tennessee

Products: Cotton, peanuts

Nickname: Heart of Dixie

Major Tourist Attractions:
    Bellingrath Gardens
    Alabama Space and Rocket Center in Huntsville
    Mound State Monument (NativeAmerican Burial Grounds)
    Jefferson Davis House in Montgomery

Land Area: 50,750 square miles

Population 2006: 5,600,000

Motto: We Dare Defend Our Rights

Trivia

- A 33-foot-tall chair is found in Anniston, Alabama.

- A monument to the boll weevil is found in Enterprise, Alabama.

- Fort Payne, Alabama, is called the "Sock Capital of the World."

Alabama Booktalks

The Watsons Go to Birmingham—1963, by Christopher Paul Curtis. Delacorte, 1995.

Enter the world of ten-year-old Kenny and his family, the Weird Watsons of Flint, Michigan. There's Momma, Dad, little sister Joey, Kenny, and Byron, who's thirteen and an "official juvenile delinquent." When Momma and Dad decide it's time for a visit to Grandma, the Watsons set out on a trip like no other. They are heading to Birmingham, Alabama, toward one of the darkest moments in American history. Momma prepares ample food for the trip because Negroes are not allowed in many restaurants. The trip becomes tedious, as Dad plans to drive eighteen hours straight through. A stop at a rest stop surrounded by dark mountains is scary.

The Watsons arrive in Birmingham and are greeted by Grandma, who gives Byron directions to the store, sends him off for food, and orders everyone else around. The church is bombed and Kenny, finding Joey's shoe, thinks she has died. He sees other dead and injured children. When he returns home and finds Joey, he tells her how much he loves her. The Watsons return to Flint, where Kenny retreats behind the couch. He is traumatized by the sights he has witnessed and ashamed that he ran from the church when he found the shoe. Byron convinces him that the bombing and the tragedies that followed were not Kenny's fault. He has nothing to be ashamed of.

Summer of the Bonepile Monster, by Aileen Kilgore. Milkweed, 1995.

Their parents are having problems and need to work things out, so Hollis and his sister, Lou, are sent to their great-grandmother's house in rural Alabama. There they experience a suspenseful summer as they investigate Bonepile Hollow, a place filled with bones of prehistoric whales. Despite a warning that "nothing that goes in the Hollow ever comes out," Hollis continues his investigation and discovers that the so-called monster of the forest is quite human. Hollis receives a further shock when he discovers his own family's involvement in the bonepile horror.

Run Away Home, by Patricia McKissack. Scholastic, 1997.

It is 1888 in Alabama when eleven-year-old Sarah Crossman sees an Apache boy escape from a train taking him to a reservation. She vows never to betray him. But after mama finds Sarah in the barn with the boy, Sky, who is dying from swamp fever, the secret is no longer hers to keep.

Mama and Sarah nurse Sky back to health, knowing that soon he will have to be turned in to the authorities. With each passing day Mama and Papa become more and more fond of Sky.

Sarah, however, is getting tired of Sky's growing relationship with her parents. Even her dog, Buster, seems to think that Sky, not Sarah, is his master now.

The Crossmans' lives and farm are threatened by the white supremacist Knights of the Southern Order, but together with Sky they fight them off. Afterward Sarah realizes that Sky is a special part of the family. The author gives a clear picture of what life in rural Alabama was like in 1888.

$66 Summer, by John Armistead. Milkweed, 2006.

George is thirteen, and to make his dream of motorcycle ownership come true, he goes to Obadiah, Alabama, to work in his grandmother's country store for the summer. George's father is a racist, but George does not share his father's views He becomes good friends with Esther and Bennett, African Americans whose father, Staples, disappeared years earlier. They spend time together, hoping to avoid the vicious dogs as they fish on old Mr. Vorhise's property, searching for outlaw treasure, and trying to avoid the strange old woman who seems to be everywhere. As the summer progresses, clues unfold about the disappearance of Staples. More than fish is found on Mr. Vorhise's, land and the town is shattered by the discovery.

More Alabama Titles

Banks, Sam. *Under the Shadow of Wings.* Atheneum, 1997.

Collier, Kristi. *Jericho Walls.* Holt, 2006.

Curtis, Christopher Paul. *The Watsons Go to Birmingham.* Delacorte, 1995.

Davis, Ossie. *Just Like Martin.* Simon & Schuster, 1999.

Henderson, Aileen. *Hard Times for Jake Smith.* Milkweed, 2004.

Holmes, Mary. *See You in Heaven,* Raintree, 1992.

Jackson, Dave. *The Forty-Acre Swindle.* Bethany House, 2000.

Johnson, Angela *Bird.* Dial, 2004.

Key, Watt. *Alabama Moon.* Farrar, 2006.

Klise, Kate. *Deliver Us from Normal.* Scholastic, 2006.

McKissack, Pat. *Run Away Home.* Scholastic, 1997.

Miller, Sarah. *Miss Spitfire: Reaching Helen Keller.* Atheneum, 2006.

Ray, Delia. *Singing Hands.* Clarion Books, 2007

Robinett, Harriett. *Walking to the Bus-rider Blues.* Atheneum, 2000.

Wallace, Daniel. *The Watermelon King.* Houghton Mifflin, 2003.

Warner, Gertrude Chandler. *The Mystery of the Midnight Dog.* Whitman, 2001.

Alaska Fact Sheet

Capital: Juneau

Largest City: Anchorage

Entered the Union: January 3, 1959

Tree: Sitka Spruce

Flower: Forget-me-not

Bird: Willow Ptarmigan

Rivers: Kuskokwim, Yukon

Nickname: Land of the Midnight Sun

Products: Petroleum

Major Tourist Attractions:
    Klondike Gold Rush National Park
    Totem poles of Ketchikan
    Denali National Park
    Glacier Bay National Park

Land Area: 570,375 square miles

Population 2006: 670,000

Motto: North to the Future

Trivia

- The World Ice Art Championships are held in Nome every March.

- Gold was discovered in Alaska in 1896.

- Alaska was purchased from Russia in 1867 for $7.2 million.

Alaska Booktalks

Julie of the Wolves, by Jean Craighead George. HarperCollins, 1972.

Miyax, motherless and fatherless, is married off at thirteen to a dimwitted older boy. Unable to come to grips with this intolerable situation, she runs away, hoping to find her way to San Francisco and her pen pal friend, who has named her Julie. She ends up lost on the barren Alaskan tundra with very few supplies and no food.

She encounters a pack of Arctic wolves, whom she knows she must somehow convince to help her survive. Near starvation, she sprawls on the lichen-covered earth behind a frost-heave and watches them very closely, until she finally learns and understands how to communicate with them in their language. She is soon accepted by the leader of the pack, Amaroq, and with their help she is able to survive. Miyax comes to love the wolves as her family and follows them throughout their travels until they stray too close to civilization and the mighty leader, Amaroq, is shot from the air by wolf bounty hunters. Miyax is frantic; determined to save the rest of the pack, she convinces them to leave the area for safer ground. She finds she must, now make the final decision to stay with the wolves or return to civilization. Terribly disenchanted with humans because of the senseless death of her beloved friend, Amaroq, she is convinced she must stay with the wolves, but an unexpected encounter with her real father, Kapugen, whom she thought dead, changes her perspective, and she is forced to take another look at her life and where it is going.

Miyax's life has been steeped in traditional Eskimo heritage as she is forced to survive while out in the wilderness, and she does not give up hope of returning to those ways, until she sees the impossibility of them when she returns to civilization and is forced to accept that the past is gone: "the hour of the wolf and the Eskimo is over."

Dogsong, by Gary Paulsen. Simon & Schuster, 1985.

Dogsong is a three-part adventure about a fourteen-year-old Eskimo youth: "The Trance," "The Dreamrun," and "Dogsong." The youth, Russel, want to experience the life of his ancestors. He is helped by Oogruk, the ancient shaman of the Innuit village, who gives him a sled, sled dogs, and both spiritual and practical guidance. In the first half of the novel Russel dreams of being a great hunter from the ice age and experiences the harsh conditions of the Arctic region. It is here that he must use all of his wits and knowledge to survive. In the last part of the novel Russel describes his adventure in the Alaskan tundra in a seven-stanza poem.

Ghost of Spirit Bear, by Ben Mikaelsen. HarperCollins, 2008.

Cole Matthews faced death but survived on a remote Alaskan island, where he was sentenced to a year of exile after beating another boy. Now, having made peace with himself and his victim, Cole must face his biggest challenge. In a high school where hate and tension are getting close to the boiling point, the rage hiding deep within Cole begins to stir. In this sequel to *Touching Spirit Bear,* Cole must face urban survival rather than wilderness survival, where every day is a struggle.

Call of the Wild, by Jack London. Sterling Unabridged Classics, 2004.

The story begins with four-year-old Buck, half St. Bernard and half Scotch shepherd, leading a relative life of ease on Judge Miller's estate in the San Fernando Valley. To pay off a gambling debt, Manuel, the gardener, sells Buck to two strangers, and his troubles begin. He is taken to the Yukon in the frozen North and beaten into submission as he is trained to become a sled dog. The instincts of his wolf ancestors emerge as Buck fights with the lead dog for the top spot in pulling the sled. Buck adapts to the severe weather and hard workloads and begins to feel the call of the wild. When the team is sold to cruel masters, Buck is saved from a beating by John Thornton, who becomes his new master. Thornton treats Buck with kindness, and the dog and man become firm friends. They travel far into the Alaskan wilderness in search of gold, and Thornton meets his death on the trip. Buck, rather than returning to civilization, joins a pack of wolves, submitting himself completely to the call of the wild.

More Alaska Titles

Bauer, Marion Dane. *A Bear Named Trouble.* Clarion, 2005.

Bell, Joanne. *Breaking Trail* Groundwood Books, 2005.

Blake, Robert. *Swift.* Philomel, 2007.

Bodett, Tom. *Williwaw!* Knopf, 1999.

George, Jean Craighead. *Julie.* HarperCollins, 1994.

Gill, Shelley. *Kiana's Iditarod.* Sasquatch Books, 2002.

Hall, Elizabeth. *Child of the Wolves.* Random House, 1997.

Hill, Kirkpatrick. *Dancing at the Odinochka.* Margaret McElderry Books, 2005.

Hill, Kirkpatrick. *Do Not Pass Go.* Margaret McElderry Books, 2007.

Hill, Kirkpatrick. *Minuk: Ashes in the Pathway.* Pleasant Co., 2002.

Hill, Kirkpatrick. *The Year of Miss Agnes.* Atheneum, 2000.

Hobbs, Will. *Down the Yukon.* HarperCollins, 2002.

Hobbs, Will. *Wild Man Island.* HarperCollins, 2003.

Joose, Barbara. *Wind Wild Dog.* Holt, 2006.

Kittredge, Frances. *Neluk: An Eskimo Boy in the Days of Whaling Ships.* Alaska Northwest Books, 2001.

Morris, Jennifer. *Come Llamas.* Delacorte, 2005.

Shaharo, Terri. *Frozen Stiff.* Delacorte, 1998.

Skurzynski, Gloria. *Buried Alive.* National Geographic, 2003.

Capital: Phoenix

Largest City: Phoenix

Entered the Union: February 14, 1912

Tree: Palo Verde

Flower: Flower of the saguaro cactus

Bird: Cactus wren

Rivers: Colorado, Gila

Nickname: Grand Canyon State

Products: Gold, silver, and copper

Major Tourist Attractions:
    Grand Canyon
    OK Corral in Tombstone
    Tucson Desert Museum
    San Xavier del Bac Mission

Land Area: 113,996 square miles

Population 2006: 6,166,218

Motto: God Enriches

 ## Trivia

- The original London Bridge is found in Lake Havasu City.

- An ostrich festival is held yearly in Chandler.

- Oatman has an egg frying contest (on its sidewalks) every July.

From *Reading the Fifty States: Booktalks, Response Activities, and More* by Nancy Polette. Westport, CT: Libraries Unlimited. Copyright © 2009.

Arizona Booktalks

Medicine Walk, by Ardath Mayhar. Atheneum, 1985.

It was not to be a long flight, the trip to grandfather's. And they had plenty of time. Why not fly over the Petrified Forest, Burr suggested to his father, who was piloting their small plane. So the two went off their flight plan, and when the accident happened, when Burr's father had a heart attack and died after bringing the plane to a landing in a desert draw, there was no way anyone would know where to look for them.

Burr did not want to leave the plane, did not want to leave his dead father. But no one would ever find him with the plane at rest under a desert cottonwood tree in an area where they had not intended to be. If he wanted to live, he had no choice but to take the small amount of water and food aboard the plane, stored there for emergencies, and set out across the hot summer desert. There were no roads to follow, no paths, and he would have to walk at least forty miles.

In this ancient home of the Apache, he found the teachings of the Apache foreman on the family ranch coming back to him at times of danger and when he wanted to give up. Hungry, thirsty, and footsore, finally on the verge of death, it was that memory—as well as the appearance of a cougar, which he decided might, in the Apache way, be his own totemic beast—that kept him going. He might not succeed in getting anywhere, but he could not give up.

One Unhappy Horse, by C. S. Adler. Houghton Mifflin, 2001.

Twelve-year-old Jan's father has died, and her mother is doing her best to make ends meet. Dove, Jan's horse, needs an operation on its leg but there is no money to pay for the surgery. Near Jan's home is an assisted living facility where Jan has struck up a friendship with Mattie, one of the residents. Eighty-five-year-old Mattie offers to pay for Dove's operation, but Mattie's daughter may have something to say about that. Why should Mattie want to pay for the operation of a horse belonging to a young girl she barely knows? More than a horse story, this is a story about mother–daughter relationships and finding ways to deal with grief and loss.

The Righteous Revenge of Artemis Bonner, by Walter Dean Myers. HarperCollins, 1992.

In 1880 two important events took place. Catfish Grimes shot dead Ugly Ned Bonner, Uncle to Artemis Bonner, and Artemis headed west to avenge Uncle Ugly's death and find the gold mine left to him in his uncle's will. Catfish Grimes is determined not to be caught. He would also like to find the gold mine before Artemis does. But Artemis has the strength of true *determination!* He tracks Catfish from Mexico to Alaska and back again. Finally they meet in a shootout in front of the Bird Cage Saloon. Catfish yells, "When I count three, go for your gun." No sooner has he shouted "one!" than both Catfish and Artemis draw. Read *The Righteous Revenge of Artemis Bonner* to discover the exciting finish to this romp through the Old West.

Danger in the Desert, by Terri Fields. Rising Moon Press, 1997.

When mom leaves the car running to go pay for gas, the car is hijacked by a man with a gun. Brothers Scott and Robbie are in the car, which is driven out into the desert, where the hijacker meets and drives away with another man, abandoning the car and the brothers. Eleven-year-old Scott attempts to drive back to the town, but the car runs out of gas. A series of trials follows, including flash fires, wild animals, injuries, floods, heat, thirst, and fear that they will never reach civilization in time. While the boys confront both real and imaginary dangers, actual survival tactics are presented.

More Arizona Titles

Adler, C. S. *The No Place Cat.* Clarion, 2002.

Birdseye, Tom. *Tarantula Shoes.* Puffin, 1996.

Campbell, Julie. *Mystery in Arizona.* Random House, 2004.

Gutman, Dan. *The Homework Machine.* Simon & Schuster, 2006.

Hayes, Joe. *Ghost Fever.* Cinci Puntos Press, 2004.

Hobbs, Will. *Crossing the Wire.* HarperCollins, 2006.

Holmas, Stig. *Apache Pass.* Harbinger House, 1996.

Holmas, Stig. *Son of Thunder.* Harbinger House, 1993.

Kadohata, Cynthia. *Weedflower.* Atheneum 2006.

Lawson, Julie. *Arizona Charlie and the Klondike Kid.* Orca Book Publishers, 2003.

Marsden, Carolyn. *Bird Springs.* Viking, 2007.

Russell, Sharmon. *The Humpbacked Flute Player.* Knopf, 1994.

Sandin, Joan. *Coyote School News.* Henry Holt, 2003.

Skurzynski, Gloria. *Over the Edge.* National Geographic Society, 2002.

Smith, Roland. *The Last Lobo.* Hyperion, 1999.

Stewart, Jennifer. *If That Breathes Fire, We're Toast.* Holiday House, 1999.

Taylor, Theodore. *Billy the Kid.* HarperCollins, 2007.

Warner, Sally. *This Isn't About Money.* Viking, 2002.

Arkansas Fact Sheet

Capital: Little Rock

Largest City: Little Rock

Entered the Union: June 15, 1836

Tree: Pine

Flower: Apple blossom

Bird: Mockingbird

Rivers: Arkansas, Mississippi

Nickname: Natural State

Products: Bauxite, furniture

Major Tourist Attractions:
Crater of Diamonds State Park
Blanchard Springs Caverns
Stuttgart Agricultural Museum
Hot Springs National Park

Land Area: 52,068 square miles

Population 2006: 2,810,272

Motto: The People Rule

Trivia

- Only state where diamonds are mined.

- Annual World Championship Duck Calling contest in Stuttgart.

- Home to both armadillos and alligators.

Arkansas Booktalks

Summer of My German Soldier, by Bette Greene. Penguin, 2006.

During World War II German prisoners of war were placed in prison camps throughout the United States. One of these camps was in Jenkinsville, Arkansas, and this novel opens as young Patty Bergin watches with fascination as a train pulls into the station and German prisoners emerge from the cars. Like many twelve-year-olds, Patty feels that no one in her family understands her, and she strikes up an unlikely friendship with Anton, one of the German prisoners. Patty feels that she and Anton truly relate to each other, and she harbors thoughts of helping him to escape. The friendship, of course, is forbidden, as Patty is Jewish and the whole town looks upon the prisoners as Nazis. It is a summer Patty will never forget, especially when the forbidden friendship is discovered.

Falling from Grace, by Ann McNichols. Walker, 2000.

Here are finely drawn portraits of a group of people who live in the sleepy town of Prosper, Arkansas, during the Great Depression years of the 1930s. The heroine of the tale is thirteen-year-old Cassie Hill. Her older sister has left town following the suicide of her boyfriend. Cassie's father becomes distant and her Sunday School teacher stirs up trouble, but Cassie finds solace in her friendship with Jan, a young but wise Hungarian immigrant. Jan believes in only peaceful solutions to problems, and in *Falling from Grace* there are problems galore, including the Ku Klux Klan, moonshine, and the church. Here you will meet unforgettable characters who may not always find the best solutions to their problems but make a sincere effort to do so.

Queen of October, by Shelley Mickle. Workman, 1992.

Come and visit Coldwater, Arkansas, in the 1960s and meet thirteen-year-old Sally Maulden. Sally, who has low self-esteem, calling herself too boring to be loved, arrives in Coldwater to stay with her grandparents. Her parents felt it was wise to send Sally away while their divorce was thrashed out. Little did her parents guess that during this summer Sally would fall in love with an older man who is an alcoholic and become friends with a striptease artist. Other unforgettable characters in this novel include Grandfather Maulden, the town doctor, who mixes up bottles of his "Inside" medicine, and Grandmother, who takes the local newspaper editor to task over removal of an ugly outhouse that can be seen from the site of the Missionary Ladies Luncheon. Both the people and their problems in Coldwater, Arkansas, seem real and make for good reading.

Philip Hall Likes Me I Reckon Maybe, by Bette Greene. Puffin Books, 1974.

Beth Lambert has a crush on Philip Hall. He is cute and smart, and at first it doesn't bother her that he beats her in class work and just about everything else. Beth is eleven and lives in Pocahontas, Arkansas. Her dream is to become a veterinarian, but to do that she must do her very best in school. Has Philip been outshining her in academics because she has let him be first? When she does do her best and beats Philip by winning the blue ribbon in calf raising at the country fair, does this mean he won't like her any more? Follow Beth's adventures as she catches turkey thieves, is part of a mountaintop rescue, and at the same time learns to face her fear of losing Philip Hall's friendship.

More Arkansas Titles

Bealer, Alex W. *Only the Names Remain: The Cherokee and the Trail of Tears.* Little, Brown, 1972.

Bowman, Eddie. *Gravy on a Bucket Lid.* Ozark, 1998.

Greene, Bette. *I've Already Forgotten Your Name, Philip Hall!* HarperCollins, 2004.

Kilgore, James. *The Passage.* Peachtree, 2006.

Lucas, Eileen. *Cracking the Wall.* Carolrhoda, 1997.

Rubright, Lynn. *Mama's Window.* Lee & Low Books, 2005.

Sargent, Dave. *Ulas, Oscar, and the Buzzard.* Ozark, 1996.

Traylor, Betty. *Buckaroo.* Delacorte, 1999.

California Fact Sheet

Capital: Sacramento

Largest City: Los Angeles

Entered the Union: September 9, 1850

Tree: Redwood

Flower: Golden poppy

Bird: California quail

Rivers: Sacramento, Colorado

Nickname: Golden State

Products: Farm crops, high tech industries

Major Tourist Attractions:
Disneyland
Yosemite National Park
Redwood Highway
Death Valley National Monument

Land Area: 155,973 square miles

Population 2006: 336,457,549

Motto: Eureka!

Trivia

- A 2,500-year-old sequoia grows in California.

- Called the vegetable capital of the world.

- Both the lowest and highest points in the continental U.S. are found here.

- The National Yo Yo Museum is located in Chico.

From *Reading the Fifty States: Booktalks, Response Activities, and More* by Nancy Polette. Westport, CT: Libraries Unlimited. Copyright © 2009.

California Booktalks

The Ballad of Lucy Whipple, by Karen Cushman. Clarion, 1996.

California Morning Whipple (who wants to be called Lucy) is unhappy. Her mother has taken the family from Massachusetts to the California gold country. There they find a ramshackle mining town and rough miners. Lucy's mother finds work in a boarding house and Lucy has one ambition . . . to get back home to Massachusetts.

She bakes and sells pies to earn money for her goal. She survives a cold and lonely winter, sees her brother almost drown, makes a good friend, suffers the death of her brother, and sees the town destroyed by fire. Through both triumph and tragedy Lucy discovers that Lucky Diggins, the mining town she wanted so much to leave, has become her home.

The Higher Power of Lucky, by Susan Patron. Simon & Schuster, 2006.

Ten-year-old Lucky's mother died when she was eight, and she was abandoned by her father, who wanted nothing to do with the child. His first wife, Brigette, becomes Lucky's guardian. But Brigitte wants to go back to France, leaving Lucky to consider running away from Hard Pan, California (population forty-three) to avoid being abandoned at some orphanage in Los Angeles where her beloved dog, HMS Beagle, won't be allowed. She'll have to lose her friends Miles, who lives on cookies, and Lincoln, future U.S. president (maybe) and member of the International Guild of Knot Tyers. As Lucky searches for her higher power, she listens around town to various anonymous meetings where people talk about hitting bottom before they can find that power to rise. But she hadn't planned on a dust storm. Or needing to lug the world's heaviest survival-kit back-pack into the desert. The people of Hard Pan do find her, and when she returns home, Brigitte tells her that she will legally adopt her.

Island of the Blue Dolphins, by Scott O'Dell. Houghton Mifflin, 1960.

Karana, a young Indian girl, lives with her family on an island in the Pacific Ocean. As she and her brother Ramo gather roots and herbs, they are ever watchful for the enemy Aleut ships and the fierce warriors that are a threat to their peaceful tribe. When danger threatens, Karana hides in the ravine behind the thick toyan bushes. With the death of Karana's father, Chief Chowig, a large ship comes to the island to take the people away. When Karana realizes that Ramo is not on the ship, she jumps into the water and swims back to the abandoned island. Ramo is killed by wild dogs, and Karana must survive alone. She makes crude weapons and gathers shellfish, abalones, and water. She builds a house on the headland and constructs a fence, held together by strands of bull kelp and sinew. But strangely enough, as the years pass Karana slowly makes friends with the leader of the wild dog pack, Rontu. And then the day comes when the Aleut ship approaches once again!

Lupita Mañana, by Patricia Beatty. HarperCollins, 2000.

Lupita loses her father in a fishing boat accident tin the waters near the small Mexican village where they live. There is no money or any way to earn a living, so Lupita and her brother must go to the United States to earn money for the family. They must face the dangers of smuggling themselves across the border, the hard labor they must endure, and the difficulty of learning a new language. And always there are the immigration officials, who are on the lookout for illegal immigrants. Despite the challenges Lupita and her brother face in struggling to survive, Lupita never loses her belief that there will be a better tomorrow.

More California Titles

Bildner, Phil. *The Greatest Game Ever Played.* Putnam, 2006.

Carey, Janet Lee. *The Double Life of Zoe Flynn.* Atheneum, 2004.

Collard, Sneed B. *Dog Sense.* Peachtree, 2005.

Ellison, James. *Akeeah and the Bee.* Newmarket Press, 2006.

Fleischman, Sid. *Bandit's Moon.* Greenwillow, 1999.

Fleischman, Sid. *The Giant Rat of Sumatra.* Greenwillow Books, 2005.

Hopkinson, Deborah. *Into the Firestorm: A Novel of San Francisco, 1906.*
   Alfred A. Knopf, 2006.

Karwoski, Gail. *Quake! A Disaster in San Francisco, 1906.* Peachtree, 2004.

Mackall, Dandi. *Rudy Rides the Rails: A Depression Era Story.* Sleeping Bear Press,
   2007.

McDonald Megan. *Julie Tells Her Story.* American Girl Publishers, 2007.

Ritter, John H. *The Boy Who Saved Baseball.* Puffin, 2005.

Robinett, Harriet. *Twelve Travelers, Twenty Horses.* Atheneum, 2003.

Smith, D. J. *The Boys of San Joaquin.* Atheneum, 2005.

Spurr, Elizabeth. *Surfer Dog.* Dutton, 2004.

Turner, Ginger. *Gold Mine! The California Gold Rush Story.* Gossamer Books, 2005.

Yep, Laurence. *The Earth Dragon Awakes: The San Francisco Earthquake of 1906.*
   HarperCollins, 2006.

Yep, Laurence. *The Journal of Wong Ming-Chung: A Chinese Miner.* Scholastic, 2000.

Colorado Fact Sheet

Capital: Denver

Largest City: Denver

Entered the Union: August 1, 1876

Tree: Colorado blue spruce

Flower: Rocky Mountain columbine

Bird: Lark bunting

Rivers: Arkansas, Colorado

Nickname: Centennial State

Products: Farm crops, cattle, sheep, gold and silver mines

Major Tourist Attractions:
Mesa Verde National Park
Bent's Old Fort near La Luna
Air Force Academy
Death Valley National Monument

Land Area: 104,094 square miles

Population 2006: 4,550,688

Motto: Nothing Without Providence

 ## Trivia

- Boulder is the only U.S. city with a glacier.

- Rocky Ford is the sweet melon capital of the world.

- The only state in the U.S. where four states come together.

- The Garden of the Gods was created by volcanoes more than 50 million years ago.

Colorado Booktalks

The Good Dog, by Avi. Aladdin Paperback, 2003.

McKinley, the head dog in the town of Steamboat Springs, Colorado, is aware of the female wolf who makes tracks around the town. The she-wolf is trying to make contact with the town dogs to help in increasing her pack, even though she finds their domestic lifestyle contemptible. McKinley's pup, Jack, wants to become a part of the wolf pack, and McKinley is torn between protecting his pup and joining his wild ancestors himself. McKinley realizes that he must find a way to keep his human master away from a wolf hunt, help a greyhound escape from its master, and hide the she-wolf when she is injured. To complicate matters, McKinley gets in trouble by stealing meat from his human family to feed the wolf. The tale ends with a face-off with the hunters and a breath-taking escape. This is a must-read for dog lovers!

Beardance, by Will Hobbs. Simon & Schuster, 2004.

Cloyd Atcitty believes that the last of the grizzlies in Colorado has disappeared. Cloyd sees the disappearance of the natural wildlife as an American tragedy. He accepts an offer by Walter, an elderly rancher friend, to join him on a trip to the mountains in search of a cache of Spanish Gold. On the trip they meet a hunter who tells them about a mother grizzly and her three cubs sighted in the high country. Cloyd sets out to find the grizzlies. When he does, the cubs are orphaned, and Cloyd is determined to stay in the mountains alone to keep the cubs alive. Here is an adventure story set high up on the Continental Divide that is sure to be a page turner. Although the books do not have to be read in order, this story is the sequel to *Bearstone,* which also features Cloyd and his concern for saving native wildlife.

The Coach That Never Came, by Patricia Beatty. HarperCollins, 1985.

When thirteen-year-old Paul Braun arrives from the East to visit his grandmother in Colorado, little does he guess he will be involved in solving a ten-year-old mystery. Grandmother gives Paul a very old, heart-decorated, gold and ruby belt buckle but doesn't recall the details about the long-ago relative who had owned it. To find out more about the previous owner, Paul and his Native American friend Jay Jenkins search through the trunks in grandmother's attic. During their search they find old newspaper clippings about a stagecoach that vanished along with its passengers and $40,000 in stolen payroll money. Not long after, the belt buckle is stolen. Could the theft be related to the long ago missing money? Is someone trying to prevent the boys from unlocking the secret of the vanishing coach? How are the buckle, the vanishing coach, and the $40,000 connected? Paul is determined to find out.

The Great Turkey Walk, by Kathleen Karr. Farrar, Straus & Giroux, 2000.

Simon Green is by far the biggest third grader. He should be, after four years in the third grade. Simon is fifteen, and although his teacher may not consider him too bright, Simon figures out that if he buys 1,000 turkeys for twenty-five cents each and herds them from Missouri to Colorado, he can sell them for five dollars each. Of course, herding 1,000 turkeys 900 miles is no easy task, especially when his partners are a drunk and a runaway slave. Simon, with the help of the turkeys, manages to solve one problem after another, including herding the turkeys across a raging river and battling a swarm of locusts. To complicate matters, Simon and his companions are followed by Simon's no-good father, a strong man who sees dollar signs in those turkeys. From the Missouri River to Denver, the action never stops in this fun Wild West adventure.

More Colorado Titles

Avi. *The Secret School.* Harcourt, 2001.

Ayres, Katherine. *Silver Dollar Girl.* Delacorte, 2000.

Bograd, Larry. *Colorado Summer.* Gareth Stevens, 1999.

Carbone, Elisa. *Last Dance on Holladay Street.* Knopf, 2005.

Creel, Ann Howard. *Nowhere, Now Here.* American Girl, 2000.

George, Jean Craighead. *River Rats, Inc.* Dutton, 1979.

Hahn, Mary Downing. *The Gentleman Outlaw and Me—Eli: A Story of the Old West.* Clarion, 1996.

Hobbs, Will. *River Thunder.* Delacorte, 1997.

Jones, J. Sydney. *Frankie.* Lodestar/Dutton, 1997.

Lottridge, Celia Barker. *The Wind Wagon.* Silver Burdett, 1995.

Oswald, Nancy. *Nothing Here but Stones.* Holt, 2004.

Roy, Ron. *Avalanche!* Dutton, 1981.

Turner, Barbara. *Treasure in Ghost Town.* Bonneville Books, 2001.

Wyss, Thelma Hatch. *Bear Dancer: The Story of a Ute Girl.* Margaret McElderry Books, 2000.

Connecticut Fact Sheet

Capital: Hartford

Largest City: Bridgeport

Entered the Union: January 9, 1788

Tree: White Oak

Flower: Mountain laurel

Bird: Robin

Rivers: Connecticut, Housatonic, Thames

Nickname: Constitution State

Products: Manufacturing, insurance industry

Major Tourist Attractions:
Whitfield House in Guilford
Mark Twain House and Museum
Mystic Seaport in Mystic
Shore Line Trolley Museum in East Haven
The Nut Museum in Lima

Land Area: 5,543 square miles

Population 2006: 3,483,400

Motto: He Who Transplanted Still Sustains

Trivia

- The U.S. Constitution was modeled after Connecticut's laws.

- The first American cookbook was published in Hartford in 1796.

From *Reading the Fifty States: Booktalks, Response Activities, and More* by Nancy Polette. Westport, CT: Libraries Unlimited. Copyright © 2009.

Connecticut Booktalks

The Witch of Blackbird Pond, by Elizabeth George Spear. Dell Publishing, 1958.

The year is 1687, and Kit Tyler is an adventurous young woman who has lived all her life on the Island of Barbados, where she was able to run free and grew up with few restrictions. But after her grandfather dies she is sent to live with her mother's sister in America. She boards a trading ship bound for Connecticut and instantly feels at home among the sailors. When the ship arrives, Kit is so excited that she cannot wait for the ship to make it to shore. She jumps on board one of the small boats, and she and several other passengers paddle to shore. One small girl drops her doll over the side of the boat, and Kit jumps into the water to rescue it. When she reaches the boat, she finds that her rash action has created displeasure among those watching. Kit's new life is filled with doing chores and attending Meeting, the long Puritan service. Her life is made more bearable when she is befriended by the Widow Tupper, who is also suspected by the townspeople of being a witch. Kit has much to learn and many challenges to face if she is ever to find happiness in this strange new world.

Windcatcher, by Avi. HarperCollins, 1992.

Eleven-year-old Tony Souza is excited. He will be able to learn to sail and take to the water with the sailboat he has bought with his paper route money. All this happens when he arrives on the Connecticut shore to spend the summer with his grandmother. A story about buried treasure intrigues both Tony and grandmother, and as Tony follows clues to the treasure, he meets a couple who are illegally diving. Not only do they refuse to answer Tony's call for help when he has lost his earnings, they attack his boat to drive him away. When Tony finally puts together all of the clues to the whereabouts of the treasure, he is captured by the couple, but is rescued in an exciting climax. Here is a modern adventure story that blends the past with the present.

My Brother Sam Is Dead, by James Lincoln Collier and Christopher Collier. Four Winds Press, 1974.

"We've beaten the British in Massachusetts! The Minutemen hid in the fields along the roads and massacred them all the way back to Boston!"

When Tim's brother Sam burst in with the exciting news, everyone in the little crossroads tavern sat silent and shocked. Most people in that part of Connecticut were Tories or people who thought the colonies had some legitimate complaints against England, but nothing serious enough to shed blood over.

Tim's father and mother, who ran the tavern, felt the same way. But not Sam. At sixteen, just a few years older than Tim, he was bull-headed. Sam was convinced that the rebel cause was just—and worth fighting for.

Tim was eager to hear more about what had happened, but he dreaded what he knew would be a bad argument between Sam and his father. Tim wondered if there was any way their disagreement would ever be settled.

A few days later, when Sam stole his father's gun and, despite Tim's efforts to stop him, went off to fight the British, Tim's fears were confirmed. To find out what happens to Sam and Tim and their mother and father, as even the peaceful Tory town of Redding Ridge is caught up in the bitter turmoil, read *My Brother Sam Is Dead.*

Through the Lock, by Carol Otis Hurst. Houghton Mifflin, 2001.

Etta has been separated from her brother and sister since each was sent to separate foster homes in 1840. Etta runs away, determined to find her family, and seeks food and shelter in what she believes to be an empty cabin. The cabin is occupied by another runaway, Walter, who has escaped from his alcoholic father. Etta gets involved with Walter's problems, which include moving a body up a mountain in the dark of night and catching vandals who attempt to sabotage the canal. Etta, Walter, and another boy must convince authorities to let them operate the lock of a new canal in order to find living quarters for the three and Walter's mother. Through all of the adventures, Etta does not lose sight of her ultimate goal: to find a home for herself, her brother, and her sister so that they can again be a family.

More Connecticut Titles

Barkan, Joanne. *A Pup in King Arthur's Court*. Gareth Stevens, 2000.

Collier, James Lincoln. *The Bloody Country*. Scholastic, 1976.

Collier, James Lincoln. *War Comes to Willie Freeman*. Delacorte, 1983.

Cooney, Caroline. *Burning Up*. Laurel-Leaf Books, 2001.

Dalgliesh, Alice. *The Courage of Sarah Noble*. Atheneum, 1954. Reissued 2008.

dePaola, Tomie. *26 Fairmont Avenue*. Putnam, 1999.

Duble, Kathleen. *Hearts of Iron*. Margaret McElderry Books, 2006.

Estes, Eleanor. *The Middle Moffat*. Harcourt, 1942.

Estes, Eleanor. *The Moffats*. Harcourt, 1941.

Estes, Eleanor. *The Moffat Museum*. Harcourt, 1983. Reissued 2001.

Estes, Eleanor. *Rufus M*. Harcourt, 1943. Reissued 2001.

Ketchum, Lisa. *Where the Great Hawk Flies*. Clarion, 2005.

Konigsburg, E. L. *From the Mixed Up Files of Mrs. Basil E. Frankweiler*. Atheneum, 2002.

L'Engle, Madeline. *An Acceptable Time*. Laurel-Leaf Books, 1989.

Lenski, Lois. *Phoebe Fairchild*. Lippincott, 1936.

Mead, Alice. *Junebug*. Farrar, 1995.

Meyer, Carolyn. *Jubilee Journey*. Harcourt, 1999.

Rinaldi, Ann. *The Education of Mary: A Little Miss of Color*. Hyperion, 2000.

Van Leeuwen, Jean. *Hannah of Fairfield*. Dial, 1999.

Van Leeuwen, Jean. *Hannah's Helping Hands*. Phyllis Fogelman Books, 1999.

Van Leeuwen, Jean. *Hannah's Winter of Hope*. Phyllis Fogelman Books, 2000.

Delaware Fact Sheet

Capital: Dover

Largest City: Wilmington

Entered the Union: December 7, 1787

Tree: Holly

Flower: Peach blossom

Bird: Blue hen chicken

Rivers: Delaware, Mispillion, Nanticoke

Nickname: Diamond State

Products: Agricultural chemicals, banking and financial services

Major Tourist Attractions:
Fort Delaware on Pea Patch Island
Hagley Museum near Wilmington
Town of New Castle
Henry Francis du Pont Winterthur Museum near Wilmington

Land Area: 2,289 square miles

Population 2006: 817,500

Motto: Liberty and Independence

Trivia

- First state to approve the U.S. Constitution.

- Raises 250 million broiler chickens every year.

- Yearly contest held in Sussex County each year to see who can launch a pumpkin the greatest distance.

Delaware Booktalks

*A **Light in the Storm: The Civil War Diary of Amelia Martin, Fenwick Island, Delaware, 1861,*** by Karen Hesse. Dear America Series. Hyperion, 1999.

Amelia Martin is fifteen and lives in the border state of Delaware. She records in her diary the events of 1861, the beginning year of the Civil War. Just as the people of Delaware are divided in their loyalties, with friends no longer speaking and businesses losing customers, Amelia's parents are also divided and facing separation fueled by the issue of slavery. Amelia works as a teacher and helps her father, who is the lighthouse keeper on Fenwick Island. Amelia's daily life in the midst of the country's struggle is revealed, as are her own struggles to clarify her thinking about secession and slavery. Here is an excellent introduction to a difficult and divisive time in American history.

*Come **Morning,*** by Leslie Davis Guccione. Lerner, 1997.

Freedom Newcastle is twelve years old. His father is now a free man but had been a slave. The year is 1850, and as Freedom works in the fields with his father, Nehemiah, he asks questions about the Underground Railroad. His father's answers are short and give no information, for Freedom's father believes that safety lies in ignorance. Then the day comes when Nehemiah is taken by two patrollers to the magistrate's court. The family's house is torched, and Freedom finds himself taking on his father's role as a conductor on the Underground Railroad. He must find a way to move a runaway slave family to the next station. But because he has been kept in ignorance, he knows little of how the Underground Railroad operates. As he uses his wits and courage to accomplish the task, he comes to appreciate the abolitionists' goal of freedom for all.

Hill Hawk Hattie, by Clara Clark. Candlewick, 2004.

The year is 1833, and eleven-year-old Hattie feels she has lost both her parents. Since her mother died, her father has become someone she hardly knows. The father she had always known as loving and caring has become gruff and at times almost mean. The mean streak must be catching, for Hattie feels mean inside, too. To please her father, Hattie cuts her hair and dresses like a boy. Pa makes her part of the crew to travel by raft in moving logs down the Delaware River from New York to Philadelphia. The Hill Hawkers who accompany them don't know that Hattie is a girl. Hattie's one consolation after enduring daily criticism from her father and the dangers of the river is her mother's diary. Her mother's words bring her a measure of comfort, and as her river adventures unfold, she records them in the diary.

Moon of the Two Dark Horses, by Sally Keehn. Philomel, 1995.

Coshmoo is the twelve-year-old son of Queen Esther, head of the Delaware tribe. Daniel is a young boy living nearby with the white settlers. The two boys are best of friends, but war clouds hover over the settlement. The year is 1776. The nation is revolting against the British, and the British urge the Delaware tribe to join them in defeating the upstart settlers. Coshmoo's dreams of a bear that can never be satisfied symbolize the plight of the Native Americans. No matter who wins the war, they are very likely to lose their land. Coshmoo and Daniel set off together to a forbidden, sacred land in an attempt to bring about peace, but their efforts only make things worse. At one point in the story Daniel is captured by the British-controlled Iroquois and forced to run the gauntlet. As hostilities increase, the strong friendship of the two boys is put to the ultimate test.

More Delaware Titles

Cheripko, Jan. *Voices of the River.* Boyds Mills, 1993.

Durrant, Lynn. *The Beaded Moccasins: The Story of Mary Campbell.* Clarion, 1998.

Nemeth, Sally. *The Heights and the Depths and Everything in Between.* Knopf, 2006.

Osborne, Mary Pope. *Revolutionary War on Wednesday.* Random House, 2000.

Osborne, Mary Pope. *Standing in the Light.* Scholastic, 1998.

Rodowsky, Colby. *Spindrift.* Farrar, Straus & Giroux, 2000.

Zeises, Lara M. *Contents Under Pressure.* Laurel Leaf, 2004.

Florida Fact Sheet

Capital: Tallahassee

Largest City: Jacksonville

Entered the Union: March 13, 1845

Tree: Sabal palm

Flower: Orange blossom

Bird: Mockingbird

Rivers: St. John's, St. Mary's, Suwannee, Apalachicola

Nickname: Sunshine State

Products: Citrus fruits

Major Tourist Attractions:
St. Augustine, founded in 1565
Walt Disney World in Orlando
John F. Kennedy Space Center
Everglades National Park

Land Area: 54,153 square miles

Population 2006: 18,100,900

Motto: In God We Trust

 ## Trivia

- Has two rivers with the name Withlacoochee.

- Venice, Florida, is the shark tooth capital of the world.

- The National Puppetry Festival is held each year in Tampa.

From *Reading the Fifty States: Booktalks, Response Activities, and More*
by Nancy Polette. Westport, CT: Libraries Unlimited. Copyright © 2009.

Florida Booktalks

Strawberry Girl, by Lois Lenski. Lippincott, 1945.

The old Roddenberry house had been empty for a long, long time but has recently come alive. It is the new home of the Boyer family. The old place has been painted and patched. Gourds filled with posies hang from the front porch. Strawberry vines have been set out. They will yield a good crop come January. Ten-year-old Birdie has even planted amaryllis bulbs in the yard. It is truly a fine beginning in their new Florida home for the Boyers, that is, until their neighbors, the Slaters, start the trouble. Pa Slater drinks a lot and lets his cattle and hogs run wild. The first time those rooters tear up the strawberry patch, Pa gives Mr. Slater a warning. And now they are at it again! Birdie is awakened by the hogs squealing and snorting. It is late at night. She hears the door slam and knows her father is after them. Birdie covers her ears as the yells and squeals and grunts grow to a deafening roar. Then silence. The girl lets out a long breath. At least Pa hasn't killed them, she thinks. At that moment the night air is split by the loud squeal of a single hog. Birdie shivers, knowing for sure now that there is trouble ahead. She is right. A few days later the Boyers find a piece of ragged white paper tacked up on their porch. It says: WILL GIT YOU YET JUST YOU WATE.

The Talking Earth, by Jean Craighead George. HarperCollins, 1983.

Billie Wind looks into the dark eyes of the medicine man. "It is told," he says, "that you do not believe in animal gods who talk; or the great serpent who lives in the Everglades and punishes bad Seminoles; or the small people who live underground and play tricks on our people. We are disturbed by your doubts." Billie wants to giggle, but the faces of the tribal council are stern. "What do you think would be a suitable punishment?" the Medicine man asks. Billie tries to think of something so dangerous and ridiculous that they will not let her do it. She looks at the Medicine Man. "I should go into the Everglades," she says, "and stay until I hear the animals talk, see the serpent and meet the little people who live underground." "Good," is the reply, much to Billie's surprise. And so begins a journey in which Billie must battle fire, wild animals, and her own prejudices before she discovers what her ancestors have long known, that the earth does indeed talk to those wise enough to listen.

Shadows in the Water, by Kathryn Lasky. Harcourt Brace, 1992.

Telepathy is nothing new to the Starbuck family. All four Starbuck twins can teleflash—talk to each other without saying a word aloud. But when the family moves to the Florida Keys to track down toxic-waste polluters, Liberty and July begin to get mysterious telekinetic messages from the deep waters of the Gulf of Mexico. Beginning as faint clicks in their minds, the messages grow stronger as the twins watch dolphins weave through the surf and leap above the waves. Could the dolphins be trying to talk to them?

In the second Starbuck Family Adventure, the Starbuck twins encounter the fascinating creatures of the tropics, from dolphins and sea turtles to crocodiles, as they set out to solve an ecological mystery that could spell disaster for the Florida Keys.

Because of Winn-Dixie, by Kate DiCamillo. Candlewick Press, 2000.

India Opal, Opal for short, and her preacher father arrive in the town of Naples, Florida. She misses her mother, who left when she was three, but tries to make the best of her new home in a trailer park. However, making friends isn't easy. Even the young people in her father's church are less than friendly. All this changes when she saves a scruffy dog at the Winn-Dixie store. The store owner is about to call the pound to take the stray away when Opal claims that the dog is hers. The dog is perfectly content to go home with Opal, and the girl soon discovers that there are friendly people in town. She meets a librarian who fought off a bear with a copy of *War and Peace.* She becomes friends with an ex-con pet store clerk who plays music to help the animals sleep. She discovers the neighborhood "witch," a blind woman who sees with her heart. Because of Winn-Dixie, the name she has given the dog, Opal is befriended by many unusual people, and her world changes and expands.

More Florida Titles

Abbott, Tony. *The Postcard.* Little, Brown, 2008.

Carter, Dorothy. *Grandma's General Store.* Farrar, Straus & Giroux, 2005.

Coman, Carolyn. *Sneaking Suspicions.* Front Street, 2007.

Corbett, Sue. *Free Baseball.* Dutton, 2006.

Creech, Sharon. *Ruby Holler.* HarperCollins, 2003.

Crocker, Carter. *The Tale of the Swamp Rat.* Philomel, 2003.

Davis, Michele Ivy. *Evangeline Brown and the Cadillac Motel.* Dutton, 2004.

DeFelice, Cynthia. *The Missing Manatee.* Farrar, Straus & Giroux, 2005.

Diterlizzi, Tony. *The Nixie's Song.* Simon & Schuster, 2007.

Farley, Walter. *The Black Stallion Challenged.* Random House, 2002.

Flood, Pansie Hart. *Sometime Friend.* Carolrhoda Books, 2005.

Grippando, James. *Leapholes.* ABA Publishing, 1958. Reissued 2006.

Harlow, Joan. *Blown Away.* Atheneum, 2007.

Hiaasen, Carl. *Flush.* Knopf, 2005.

Hiaasen, Carl. *Hoot.* Knopf, 2002.

Holt, Kimberly. *Harper Reed, Navy Brat.* Holt, 2007.

Jordan, Rosa. *Lost Goat Lane.* Peachtree, 2004.

McDonald, Joyce. *Devil on My Heels.* Laurel Leaf Books, 2005.

Myers, Anna. *Flying Blind.* Walker, 2003.

Peck, Robert Newton. *Horse Thief: A Novel.* HarperCollins, 2002.

Rubel, Nicole. *It's Hot and Cold in Miami.* Farrar, Straus & Giroux, 2006.

Waters, Zack C. *Blood Moon Rider.* Pineapple Press, 2006.

Woods, Brenda. *My Name Is Sally Little Song.* Putnam, 2006.

Georgia Fact Sheet

Capital: Atlanta

Largest City: Atlanta

Entered the Union: ~~March 3, 1845~~ Jan. 2, 1788

Tree: Live Oak

Flower: Cherokee Rose

Bird: Brown thrasher

Rivers: Chattahoochee, Savannah, Suwanneea

Nickname: Peach State and Empire State of the South

Products: Agriculture, timber, textiles

Major Tourist Attractions:
Dahlonega Gold Museum
Torah Mounds
Okefenokee National Wildlife Refuge
Little White House in Warm Springs

Land Area: 59,425 square miles

Population 2006: 8,700,700

Motto: Wisdom, Justice, and Moderation

Trivia

- Confederate hero statues are carved our of the granite of Stone Mountain.

- Rebecca Felton, the first U.S. woman senator, came from Georgia.

- Champion weightlifter Paul Anderson came from Georgia. He lifted 6,000 pounds.

Georgia Booktalks

Kira Kira, by Cynthia Kadohata. Atheneum, 2004.

Lynn Takeshima shows little sister Katie the beauty found in the world by labeling even the most common things, like a box of tissues, "Kira-Kira." Things that are deep but can be seen through at the same time, like the sky, the ocean, and people's eyes, are Kira-Kira. Lynn is a true big sister. When father's small shop fails, the family must move from their Japanese community in Iowa to Georgia, where there are few Japanese families. Katie does not understand why people stare and classmates ignore her. The Takeshima family is a very traditional and honorable family, and Katie is taught from birth that lying and stealing are wrong. When Lynn contracts a fatal illness, the whole family has difficulty coping. Katie lies to her teacher about her absences from school to care for Lynn. She steals nail polish from the store because she has no money to buy it for Lynn. But it is Lynn who teaches Katie to look beyond tomorrow. When Lynn dies, it is Katie who proves that there will be a brighter future.

This is a touching novel that deals with poverty and prejudice, with dreams and accomplishments, and most of all with hope.

Football Genius, by Tim Green. HarperCollins, 2007.

Twelve-year-old Troy White has a phenomenal gift. He can predict any football play before it happens. When his single mom gets a job with the Atlanta Falcons, Troy figures he has a chance to help his favorite team, and to get bully Jamie Renfro off his back about their losing streak. With the help of his two best friends, Tate, a feisty, talented girl who's a great kicker, and steady, solid Nathan, Troy is determined to prove just how much the Falcons need him on board,

From the suspense of Troy's decision to get into star linebacker Seth Halloway's exclusive compound to his excitement at standing in the middle of the action on a football field, this is a nonstop story of one boy's struggle to realize his dreams.

Sounder, by William Armstrong. HarperCollins, 1969.

Sounder, the great coon dog, has the neck and shoulders of a bulldog and the melodious bay of a hound. When he trees a coon, his voice rolls through the moonlit night and across the flatlands, louder then any dog's in the whole countryside. But Sounder cannot save his master—the poor black sharecropper driven to steal for his hungry wife and children. Sounder cannot save him from the sheriff's posse, nor can he save him from fate.

For fate pursues them both, master and coon dog, mauling each of them in its cruel, impersonal jaws, while the boy who loves the two of them is forced to bear his sorrow like a man, although he is still a child.

The power of William H. Armstrong's prose and James Barkley's illustrations quite simply speaks for itself. And though the story burns with indignation, it climbs to moments of nobility and resignation that return, in memory, like a final benediction or the closing of a song.

Freedom Train, by Evelyn Coleman. Margaret McElderry Books, 2008.

Clyde Thomason is proud to have an older brother who guards the Freedom Train. It is 1947, and the train is traveling to all forty-eight states, carrying important documents such as the Declaration of Independence and the Bill of Rights. Clyde is lucky that the train is stopping in Atlanta. In the segregated South the train will only stop in cities that agree to integrate the crowds lining up to see its famous contents.

Clyde has been chosen to recite the Freedom Pledge, but he's afraid he'll chicken out. When the class bully tries to beat him up, William, an African American boy, comes to his rescue. Clyde is amazed but finds he can be open about his friendship with William. Then William's family is threatened, and Clyde must make a choice. Will he have the courage to speak out to defend William's freedom?

More Georgia Titles

Amateau, Gigi. *Claiming Georgia Tate.* Candlewick, 2005.

Bradley, Kimberly. *Halfway to the Sky.* Delacorte, 2002.

Brady, Laurel. *Say You Are My Sister.* HarperCollins, 2001.

Bryant, Jennifer. *Pieces of Georgia.* Knopf, 2006.

Dashner, James. *A Door in the Woods.* Bonneville Books, 2003.

Dudley, David. *The Bicycle Man.* Clarion, 2005.

Going, K. L. *The Liberation of Gabriel King.* Putnam, 2005.

Hoffman, Mary. *Stravaganza: City of Flowers.* Bloomsbury, 2005.

Kudlinski, Kathleen. *The Spirit Catchers.* Watson-Guptill, 2004.

Matthews, Kezi. *Scorpio's Child* Cricket Books, 2001.

Mosley, Walter. *47.* Little, Brown, 2005.

Murphy, Rita. *Night Flying.* Delacorte, 2000.

Myracal, Lauren. *Thirteen.* Dutton, 2008.

O'Connor, Barbara. *Fame and Glory in Freedom, Georgia.* Frances Foster Books, 2003.

O'Connor, Barbara. *Moonpie and Ivy.* Farrar, Straus & Giroux, 2001.

Porter, Pamela. *Sky.* Groundwood Books, 2004.

Rinaldi, Ann. *Numbering All the Bones.* Hyperion, 2002.

Siegelson, Kim. *The Trembling Earth.* Philomel, 2004.

Woods, Brenda. *My Name Is Sally Littlesong.* Putnam, 2006.

Hawaii Fact Sheet

Capital: Honolulu

Largest City: Honolulu

Entered the Union: August 21, 1959

Tree: Kukui

Flower: Yellow hibiscus

Bird: Hawaiian goose

Rivers: Wailuku, Anahulu

Nickname: Aloha State

Products: Coffee, pineapple, coconut

Major Tourist Attractions:
Pearl Harbor
Waikiki Beach
Waimea Canyon

Land Area: 10,932 square miles

Population 2006: 1,257,600

Motto: The Life of the Land I Perpetuated in Righteousness

Trivia

- The Hawaiian Islands were formed by undersea volcanoes.
- Hawaii is the only state that grows coffee.
- Kahului is home to the Paper Airplane Museum.
- Hilo holds an annual hula competition.

Hawaii Booktalks

In the Shadow of the Pali, by Lisa Cindrich Putnam, 2002.

Twelve-year-old Lili saw the island first. Its sheer black cliffs rose from the ocean floor like a glistening, hungry sea serpent. With a single word, leprosy, Lili was condemned to this island prison. The girl got the disease when forced by a cruel uncle to care for his mother. Lili is determined not to cry, for the anger in her heart makes her strong. But along with the other lepers in the boat, she doesn't expect a place of anarchy with no food or housing. Dark, twisted shapes on the beach meet the frightened passengers. A stumpy figure pushes forward, ratty skirt dangling from her waist. "I decide who eats!" she screams, swinging a club through the air. "The supplies are meant for everyone," Lili replies. A clawlike hand touches Lili's leg. She looks down to see a young boy. There are brown spots on his arms and face, larger than those on Lili's arms. "Don't you know," he says. "In this place there is no law." It is then that the girl knows she must survive, even if it means a face-off with the violent woman and the hungry people.

The Million Dollar Putt, by Dan Gutman. Hyperion, 2007.

Edward Bogard, Bogie for short, may be blind, but he can learn just about anything he sets his mind to: riding a bike, parasailing, and playing guitar. Even though many things come easily to him, he is stunned when he goes to a driving range and finds he has the swing of a pro. But blind golfing is a team sport, and Bogie needs a coach.

Enter Birdie, a kooky and mysterious girl next door. A bit of a loner, Birdie creates elaborate worlds in miniature in her basement and has managed to make it to age twelve without learning to ride a bike.

Someone anonymously enters Bogie in a gold tournament with a million dollar prize. If he can team up with Birdie to conquer the greens of Hawaii, could she be the unlikely key to victory?

The Broccoli Tapes, by Jan Slepian. Penguin Books, 1989.

The Davidson family moves from Boston, Massachusetts, to Hawaii, where they will live for five months. Eleven-year-olds Sara and Sam find that making new friends is not easy. They spend much of their days at the lava field at the end of their road. There they meet and become friends with Eddie Nutt, a boy from a broken family. Eddie's mother abandoned him when he was quite small. She now lives in Arizona with her new husband and wants Eddie to join her. The boy doesn't know what to do.

Sara is recording her activities in Hawaii on tape for an oral history project for her sixth-grade teacher in Boston. The children do find a surprise in the lava field, and as the end of the fifth month approaches, they must find a home for the surprise. The story is funny and touching, and readers will be delighted with the happy ending.

Lord of the Deep, by Graham Salisbury. Random House, 2003.

Thirteen-year-old Mikey works for his stepfather on a charter boat in Hawaii. Mikey calls his stepfather, Bill, "the Lord of the Deep," because the boy knows no one can match Bill as the skipper of a deep sea charter boat. As Mikey learns the many jobs required for the preparation and maintenance of a charter boat, he also spends time with his mother and younger half-brother. The calm daily routine is interrupted, however, when two crude men hire the boat for a three-day trip to catch a huge marlin. When the big catch becomes a possibility, Mikey faces a difficult choice. The reader will be right in the middle of the sports action as anglers try to land their prey. The greatest prize, however, is the close relationship between Mikey and Bill.

More Hawaii Titles

Dennenberg, Harry. *Early Sunday Morning: The Pearl Harbor Diary of Amber Billows.* Scholastic, 2001.

Ellis, Sarah. *Odd Man Out.* Groundwood Books, 2006.

Farley, Terri. *The Horse Charmer.* HarperCollins, 2007.

Frederick, Heather. *The Education of Patience Goodspeed.* Simon & Schuster, 2004.

Hossack, Sylvie. *Green Mango Magic.* Avon, 1998.

Kudlinski, Kaathleen. *Pearl Harbor Is Burning!* Viking, 1991.

Mazer, Harry. *A Boy at War: A Novel of Pearl Harbor.* Simon & Schuster, 2001.

Mazer, Harry. *A Boy No More.* Simon & Schuster, 2004.

Mullins, Vera. *Kala and the Sea Bird.* Golden, 1966.

Osborne, Mary Pope. *High Tide in Hawaii.* Random House, 2003.

Salisbury, Graham. *House of the Red Fish.* Wendy Lamb Books, 2006.

Salisbury, Graham, *Jungle Dogs.* Delacorte, 1998.

Salisbury, Graham. *Shark Bait.* Delacorte, 1997.

Skurzynski, Gloria. *Rage of Fire.* National Geographic, 1998.

Spradlin, Michael. *To Hawaii with Love.* HarperCollins, 2005.

White, Ellen. *Kaiulani, the People's Princess.* Scholastic, 2001.

Wiles, Debbie. *Love, Ruby Lavender.* Harcourt, 2003.

Winkler Henry. *Summer School, What Genius Thought That Up?* Houghton Mifflin, 2004.

Idaho Fact Sheet

Capital: Boise

Largest City: Boise

Entered the Union: July 3, 1890

Tree: White Pine

Flower: Lilac

Bird: Mountain bluebird

Rivers: Snake, Salmon, Clearwater, Kootenai

Nickname: Gem State

Products: Potatoes, sugar beets, wheat, lumber

Major Tourist Attractions:
Hell's Canyon
Nez Perce National Historical Park
Sun Valley ski resorts

Land Area: 85,570 square miles

Population 2006: 1,366,300

Motto: It Is Forever

Trivia

- Idaho has more than 25,000 farms.

- 70 percent of the people live in the southern part of the state.

- More potatoes are grown in Idaho than in any other state.

Idaho Booktalks

Bonanza Girl, by Patricia Beatty. Beech Tree, 1993.

Katherine Scott, a widow, decides to leave Portland, Oregon, with her two children for the Idaho gold fields, thinking she will make a living teaching school. "Miners do have children, don't they?" she says to her skeptical daughter, Ann Katie. When the Scott family arrives in Eagle City, Katherine discovers that if the miners pouring into Idaho have kids, they haven't brought them along. The Scotts also find that there is no place to live in Eagle City but a tent and nothing to eat but beans. With the help of an irrepressible lady from Sweden, the Scotts open a restaurant. Soon they are as much a part of the boomtown atmosphere that characterized Idaho during the 1880s as any miner, scoundrel, thief, or profiteer. And they love it!

West to the Land of Plenty: The Diary of Teresa Angelino Viscardi, New York to Idaho Territory, 1883, by Jim Murphy. Scholastic, 2002.

Moving west in 1883 meant leaving behind not only the comforts of home but all the family and friends who were so dear. The train trip was less than comfortable, with thirty wooden seats on each side of an aisle and two to a seat. Fourteen-year-old Teresa does not want to leave New York, but has no choice when her aunt and uncle decide to move the entire family to the Idaho Territory. When the train tracks end, the family joins a wagon train. News comes of the discovery of silver in the mountains, and the men of the train take off to make their fortunes. Several family members become ill with a fever, and their wagon must leave the wagon train. For the first time in her life, Teresa must fire a gun, to scare off rough-looking bandits. Despite all the troubles, the family continues on to what they believe is the land of opportunity. Teresa writes in her journal: "I think these past weeks and days have taught me that out here what you hope for is one thing but what happens is something else completely."

The Case of the Missing Cutthroats: An Ecological Mystery, by Jean Craighead George. HarperCollins, 1999.

This mystery begins when Spinner, a New York City native who would rather perform on a ballet stage than cast flies, catches the family prize in an Idaho mountain stream, much to her boy cousins' dismay. The prize fish, a huge cutthroat trout, had been thought to be extinct in the river, and Spinner and her cousin set out to solve the mystery of how this one spectacular cutthroat survived until Spinner reeled him in. As the mystery is revealed, the reader will discover how humans can have an impact on nature and how things can be fixed or changed.

The Garden of Eden Motel, by Morse Hamilton. HarperTeen, 1999.

The year is 1952, and eleven-year-old Dal reluctantly accompanies his new stepfather, Harry Sabatini, from his home in Detroit to the small town of Eden, Idaho. The name of the town turns out to be a joke, for an Eden it is not. Dal and Harry stay at the Garden of Eden Motel. Harry's job as a crop inspector keeps him busy during the day, and Dal makes friends with heavyset Wilbur and with Patty, who is ready to try anything new. Dal gets his first job and buys shares in a uranium mine. Dal and Harry draw closer together as the months pass, and goodhearted Harry slowly gains the boy's trust. When the two go to inspect the uranium mine, Harry is bitten by a rattlesnake, and through quick action Dal saves Harry's life. No longer is Harry Mr. Sabatini. To Dal he has become Dad!

More Idaho Titles

Carlton, Bea. *Secret of Windthorn.* Thorndike Press, 1987.

Craighead, Charles. *The Eagle and the River,* Durran, 1995.

Crutcher, Chris. *Running Loose.* Greenwillow, 1983.

Crutcher, Chris. *The Sledding Hill.* Geenwillow, 2005.

Farrell, Mary. *Fire in the Hotel.* Clarion, 2004.

George, Jean Craighead. *Hook a Fish, Catch a Mountain.* Dutton, 1975.

Hite, Sid. *King of the Mild Frontier.* Greenwillow, 2003.

Hite, Sid. *King of Slippery Falls.* Scholastic ,2004.

Ingold, Jeanettte. *The Big Burn.* Harcourt, 2002.

McManus, Patrick. *Never Cry "Arp."* Holt, 1996.

Patneude, David. *Colder Than Ice.* Whitman, 2003.

Wyss, Thelma. *Ten Miles from Winnemucca.* HarperColllins, 2002.

Capital: Springfield

Largest City: Chicago

Entered the Union: December 3, 1818

Tree: White oak

Flower: Violet

Bird: Cardinal

Rivers: Mississippi, Ohio, Illinois, Wabash

Nickname: Prairie State

Products: Machinery, agriculture, metal products, chemicals, published materials

Major Tourist Attractions:
Abraham Lincoln's home
Cahokia Mounds
Shawnee National Forest

Land Area: 57,914 square miles

Population 2006: 12,700,600

Motto: State Sovereignty—National Union

 ## Trivia

- The state name is a native American word meaning "Superior Men."

- The country's first skyscraper was built in Chicago in 1885.

- 100-year-old Lincoln Park Zoo has more than 1,000 animals.

- National Lawn Mower Races happen every year in Mendotta.

Illinois Booktalks

A Long Way from Chicago, by Richard Peck. Dial, 1997.

The setting is a small town in Illinois, a far cry in distance and culture from Chicago, where Joey and Mary Alice live. The brother and sister make seven summer visits to Grandma Dowdel's house from 1929 until 1936, a time when life was hard and jobs were scarce. The children, who expect a dull summer on their first visit, discover that Grandma does not fit the grandmotherly stereotype. She is spirited, ready for adventure, and up to any challenge. During their first visit they see a corpse that is not resting easy. The next summer Grandma does battle with the Cowgill boys, who are terrorizing the town. An eventful day in 1931 has the children helping Grandma trespass, poach, catch the sheriff in his underwear, and feed the hungry. Grandma not only breaks the rules, she breaks the law when she brews beer during Prohibition and steals the sheriff's boat. But as always she manages to get away with everything. The final summer of their visit brings the centennial celebration that no one will forget. Grandma makes sure that Joey and Mary Alice leave with a bang!

Across Five Aprils, by Irene Hunt. Follett, 1964.

The setting of this novel is Illinois during the Civil War. Jethro's family works a farm in Southern Illinois, and it is a family divided. One of Jethro's brothers has gone to fight for the North, and the other has left to fight for the South. The surrounding community is supporting the Union, and Jethro's family faces the scorn of those around them. Jethro must take on the responsibilities of a man when his father has a heart attack and the boy must run the farm. The boy gets reports of the war through letters and helps his cousin, a deserter from the Union Army, by writing to the president. By the end of the novel, even though he has not been on the front lines, the boy has truly experienced the horrors of war.

A Year Down Yonder, by Richard Peck. Dial, 2000.

In this sequel to *A Long Way from Chicago,* fifteen-year-old Mary Alice moves in with her grandmother for a year. The year is 1937, and the Great Depression has not yet ended. Mary Alice's father has lost his job, her parents had to move to a one-room apartment, and her brother Joey has gone out west to work for the Civilian Conservation Corps. Grandma Dowel is well known and often feared by the townsfolk. She knows how to use a rifle and has no tome for fools. She cooks up outrageous schemes, which at first Mary Alice wants no part of. However, as her year is filled with moonlit schemes, romances, and a parade of fools, Mary Alice discovers there is more of her grandmother in her than she had suspected.

The Ghost Belonged to Me, by Richard Peck. Dial, 1976.

On a small farm near Pittsfield, Illinois, young Alexander sees a strange light coming from the barn late at night. He remembers the words of his friend, Blossom Culp, when she told him that he could make contact with the unseen.

Make contact he does, for when Alex goes to the barn to investigate the light, he meets a lady ghost and her dog, who are living in the barn. The ghost warns him of great danger and helps Alex save a trolley full of people from crashing into a ravine. The ghost also helps Alex's sister avoid a terrible mistake.

To show his appreciation, Alex volunteers to take the ghost's remains to a resting place beside her family's remains. He enlists the aid of his uncle to make the trip from Illinois to Louisiana to deliver the remains to their final resting place. A fast-paced, funny ghost story!

More Illinois Titles

Anderson, Joan. *Joshua's Westward Journal*. Morrow, 1987.

Bauer, Marion Dane. *Secret of the Painted House*. Random House, 2007.

Dell, Pamela. *Liam's Watch: A Strange Story of the Chicago Fire*. Tradition Publishers, 2005.

Durrant, Lynda. *My Last Skirt: The Story of Jenny Hodges, Union Soldier*. Clarion, 2006.

Grove, Vicki. *Rimwalkers*. Putnam & Grosset, 1996.

Hart, Alison. *A Spy on the Home Front*. Pleasant Company, 2005.

Johnson, Carl. *A Diamond in the Dust*. Dial, 2001.

Ketchum, Liza. *Orphan Journey Home*. Avon Books, 2000.

Klise, Kate. *Deliver Us from Normal*. Scholastic, 2006.

Klise, Kate. *Far from Normal* Scholastic, 2005.

Matas, Crol. *Rosie in Chicago*. Aladdin, 2003.

Moranville, Shaelle. *Over the River*. Holt, 2002.

Park, Linda Sue. *Project Mulberry*. Clarion, 2005.

Peck, Richard. *Fair Weather*. Puffin, 2001.

Peck, Richard. *On the Wings of Heroes*. Dial, 2007.

Peck, Richard. *The River Between Us*. Dial, 2003.

Smith, Greg. *Ninjas, Piranhas and Galileo*. Little, Brown, 2003.

Tripp, Valerie. *Molly: An American Girl*. American Girl, 1990.

Von Ahnen, Katherine. *Heart of Naosaqua*. Roberts Rinehart, 1996.

Indiana Fact Sheet

Capital: Indianapolis

Largest City: Indianapolis

Entered the Union: December 11, 1816

Tree: Tulip tree

Flower: Peony

Bird: Cardinal

Rivers: Ohio, Wabash, White, Tippecanoe

Nickname: Hoosier State

Products: Corn, soybeans, manufacturing

Major Tourist Attractions:
Indianapolis Motor Speedway
Historic Fort Wayne
Connor Prairie Settlement in Noblesville

Land Area: 36,410 square miles

Population 2006: 6,200,700

Motto: Crossroads of America

Trivia

- Indianapolis 500, the world's greatest auto race, is held each year.

- Wabash, Indiana, was the first U.S. city to have electric lights.

- Five vice presidents have come from Indiana.

- The town of Santa Claus, Indiana, receives thousands of letters to Santa each year.

Indiana Booktalks

Here Lies the Librarian, by Richard Peck. Dial, 2006.

"Peewee" McGrath is fourteen. She thinks no one could be as wonderful as her big brother Jake. She also thinks school is a waste of time, and the best way to spend a day is helping Jake tinker with cars. The year is 1914, when most automobiles had to be cranked by hand to start. Jake's auto repair shop isn't much, but he and Peewee are hoping for the day when a real road will be built in the township, bringing lots of cars and lots of business.

Imagine their surprise when four librarians on a mission arrive from Indianapolis. Irene Ridpath, their leader, is determined to reopen the town's library, defunct for some time. Irene takes Peewee in hand to teach her how to be a lady. Another librarian, Grace, uses her knowledge of automobiles to become friends with Jake. The four work together to compete in the township's first annual and unforgettable road race. Fast action and lots of laughs make this a must read.

The Teacher's Funeral: A Comedy in Three Parts, by Richard Peck. Dial, 2004.

Miss Myrtle Arbuckle, teacher in the one-room schoolhouse, has passed away, and her pupils are not sad. Maybe this means there won't be school anymore, and fifteen-year-old Russell Culver and his friend Charlie will be free to head to the Dakotas, where they know their future lies. Unfortunately for Russell's dreams, his sister Tansey takes over as the new teacher. From the little ones to the boys taller than she is, Tansy must handle them all. Does Glenn Tarbox, who is older than the teacher, have something other than learning in mind? Is Charlie, too, captive to Tansy's charms? Who is responsible for the poems showing up all over town that reveal information some folks prefer not to have posted? Meet an unforgettable cast of characters at *The Teacher's Funeral.*

Turn Homeward, Hannalee, by Patricia Beatty. HarperCollins, 1999.

Soldiers were not the only prisoners taken during the Civil War. As Union forces invaded one Southern town after another, they closed the factories and textile mills and took women and children prisoners. They were sent north to work in factories there. Hannalee was twelve and her brother ten when they were taken prisoner and sent north to be hired out as servants or mill workers. Even the child prisoners were hated by many Northerners who had lost fathers and sons in the war. Hannalee does manage to escape. She dresses as a boy and finds her brother. The two head for home, where their mother is anxiously waiting. On their travels they witness the bloody battle of Franklin and experience the hardships of many Southerners trying to survive, so that Hannalee can keep her promise to her mother that she would return home.

Running Out of Time, by Margaret Peterson Haddix. Simon & Schuster, 1997.

Imagine living in a frontier village in Clifton, Indiana, in 1840. You and your friends were born there, and it is the only life you know. Then a terrible disease, diphtheria, hits the village, and the children are dying. It is then that thirteen-year-old Jesse Keyser learns a shocking secret from her mother. The village is an experimental village developed by unethical scientists. No one is allowed to leave, and those who view the village from the outside are unseen. The year is 1996, not 1840. Jesse's mother reveals the secret and sends the girl out of the village to bring back medical help. For Jesse, who has spent her entire life in the 1840s, life in 1996 is terribly frightening. How can she maneuver through this strange new world of cars, telephones, and television? Will she be stopped by the scientists before she can find medical help for the dying children? A fast-paced, suspenseful novel.

More Indiana Titles

Bradley, Kimberly. *One of a Kind Mallie.* Delacorte, 1999.

Collier, Kristi. *Throwing Stones.* Holt, 2006.

Crilley, M. *Billy Clikk: Rogmasher Rampage.* Delacorte, 2005.

Day, Karen. *Tall Tales.* Wendy Lamb Books, 2007.

Finlay, Martha. *Millie's Remarkable Journey.* Mission City, 2002.

Fletcher, Susan. *Dadblamed Union Army Cow.* Candlewick, 2007.

Hamilton, Kersten. *Millie's Courageous Days.* Mission City Press, 2001.

Hamilton, Kersten. *Millie's Remarkable Journey.* Mission City Press, 2002.

Hamilton, Kersten. *Millie's Unsettled Season.* Mission City Press, 2001.

Kornblatt, Matt. *Izzie's Place.* Atheneum, 2003.

Lasky, Kathryn. *Christmas After All: The Great Depression Diary of Minnie Swift.* Scholastic, 2001.

Lawler, Laurie. *School at Crooked Creek.* Holt, 2004.

Naylor, Phyllis Reynolds. *Bernie Magruder and the Bats in the Belfry.* Atheneum, 2003.

Swain, Gwenyth. *Chig and the Second Spread.* Delacorte, 2003.

Woodworth, Chris. *Georgie's Moon.* Farrar, Straus & Giroux, 2006.

Woodworth, Chris. *When Ratboy Lived Next Door.* Farrar, Straus & Giroux, 2005.

Capital: Des Moines

Largest City: Des Moines

Entered the Union: December 28, 1846

Tree: Oak

Flower: Wild rose

Bird: Eastern goldfinch

Rivers: Missouri, Mississippi, Des Moines

Nickname: Hawkeye State

Products: Corn, soybeans, hogs, farm machinery

Major Tourist Attractions:
Living History Farms near Des Moines
Floyd Monument in Sioux City
Iowa State Fair in Des Moines

Land Area: 56,272 square miles

Population 2006: 2,944,100

Motto: Our Liberties We Prize and Our Rights We Will Maintain

 **Trivia**

- Glaciers from the ice age left rich soil in Iowa.

Iowa Booktalks

Kate Shelley: Bound for Legend, by Robert San Souci. Dian, 1995.

Would you like to have a bridge named after you? Kate Shelley did. Kate was born on an Iowa farm in 1881. She was a tomboy who rode bareback and shot hawks. She often danced across the railroad bridge that spanned the roaring Des Moines River. Much of the time she plowed and planted. Kate had to run the farm because her father was dead and her mother was an invalid.

One stormy winter night in 1896, with a train due in one hour, part of the railroad bridge collapsed. Kate crawled on hands and knees across the remaining part of the icy bridge to get to town with a warning. A telegraph operator reached the train in time. Brave Kate saved the lives of all the passengers on the train. In gratitude, the state of Iowa named the new bridge after Kate.

The Princess in the Pigpen, by Jane Resh Thomas. Houghton Mifflin, 1989.

Time trek to seventeenth-century England to the bedside of the daughter of the Duke of Umberland. Elizabeth has tossed feverishly throughout the night and then awakens to find herself in the McCormick farm house in present-day Iowa. While farm families are peasants in Elizabeth's world, they do not possess magic powers as this family appears to: switching a light off and on and moving from one place to another in carriages not pulled by horses. A frightening trip to the doctor cures the girl's illness, and her encounters with the trappings of everyday life in the twenty-first century make interesting reading. Will she want to return to the seventeenth century after all she has seen and heard? Will anyone believe that that is where she came from?

Squashed, by Joan Bauer. Putnam, 2000.

In Iowa folks take agriculture prizes seriously. Ellie Morgan has grown a huge, over 600-pound pumpkin. She plans to bring it to the Harvest Fair, weigh in, and walk away with the blue ribbon. She names the pumpkin Max and treats it as if it were a person. She hovers over it during a storm and protects it from pumpkin thieves. With the help of her boyfriend and her grandma, Ellie does enter her pumpkin in the weigh-in and wins the blue ribbon, gaining the respect of her doubting father. Happiness and sadness are mixed as finally Ellie returns Max to the earth so that his seeds can grow new pumpkins.

The Stumptown Kid, by Carol Gorman. Peachtree, 2005.

In 1952 Charlie Nebraska is the only child of his mother, a widow. His father died in the Korean War, and Charlie does not like his mother's boyfriend, Vern. Charlie loves baseball but is rejected by the team he hopes to join, the Wildcats. Along comes Luther, a former player in the Negro Leagues. Charlie talks Luther into coaching the Stumptown team so that they will be able to beat the Wildcats. Luther, however, has a past. A pitch to a drunk batter who was white killed the man, and the man's brother finds Luther, seeking revenge. Vern aids Luther's attacker, showing his true colors to Charlie's mother. This is a tale of a town that is filled with prejudice yet learns acceptance. It is a tale of a strong friendship between a boy and his coach and mentor and a series of frightening events that manage to change the town's outlook.

More Iowa Titles

Horvath, Polly. *An Occasional Cow*. Farrar, 1989.

Johnston, Tim. *Never So Green*. Farrar, Straus & Giroux, 2002.

Kenny, Kathryn. *The Happy Valley Mystery*. Random House, 2004.

Kimmel, Elizabeth. *To the Frontier*. HarperCollins, 2001.

Kladstrup, Kristen. *Book of Story Beginnings*. Candlewick, 2006.

Lawler, Laura. *Addie's Forever Friend*. Whitman, 1997.

Leiberg, Carolyn. *West with Hopeless*. Dutton, 2004.

Lottridge, Celia. *Ticket to Canada*. Silver Burdett, 1996.

Matthews, Eleanor. *The Linden Tree*. Milkweed, 2007.

McCully, Emily. *Hurry*. Harcourt Race, 2000.

Pryor, Bonnie. *Luke on the Golden Trail, 1849*. William Morrow, 1999.

Rylant, Cynthia. *Old Town in the Green Groves*. HarperCollins, 2002.

Woodruff, Elvira. *Ghost of Lizard Light*. Dial, 1999.

Capital: Topeka

Largest City: Wichita

Entered the Union: January 29, 1861

Tree: Cottonwood

Flower: Sunflower

Bird: Western meadowlark

Rivers: Kansas, Republican, Smoky Hill, Arkansas, Missouri

Nicknames: Sunflower State and Jayhawk State

Products: Wheat, meat packing

Major Tourist Attractions:
   The Eisenhower Center in Abilene
   Kansas Cosmosphere and Space Center in Hutchinson
   Dodge City

Land Area: 82,277 square miles

Population 2006: 2,723,500

Motto: To the Stars Through Difficulties

 ## Trivia

- Kansas produces more wheat than any other state.

- Helium was discovered in 1905 at the University of Kansas.

- An international Pancake Day race is held each year in Liberal, Kansas.

- A ball of twine weighing more than 17,000 pounds is on display in Cawker City.

Kansas Booktalks

Rifles for Watie, by Harold Keith. Thomas Y. Crowell, 1957.

Jeff Bussey walks briskly up the rutted wagon road toward Fort Leavenworth on his way to join the Union volunteers. It is 1861 in Linn County, Kansas, and Jeff is elated at the prospect of fighting for the North at last.

In the Indian country south of Kansas there is dread in the air, and the name Stand Watie is on every tongue. A hero to the rebel, a devil to the Union man, Stand Watie leads the Cherokee Indian Nation fearlessly and successfully on savage raids behind the Union lines. Jeff comes to know the Watie men only too well.

He is probably the only soldier in the West to see the Civil War from both sides and live to tell about it. Amid the roar of cannon and the swish of flying grapeshot, Jeff learns what it means to fight in battle. He learns how it feels to never have enough to eat and to forage for his food or starve. He sees the green fields of Kansas and Oklahoma laid waste by Watie's raiding parties, homes gutted, precious corn deliberately uprooted. He marches endlessly across parched, hot land, through mud and slashing rain, always hungry, always dirty and dog-tired.

And Jeff, plain spoken and honest, makes friends and enemies. The friends are strong men like Noah Babbitt, the itinerant printer who once walked from Topeka to Galveston to see the magnolias in bloom; boys like Jimmy Lear, too young to carry a gun but old enough to give up his life at Cane Hill; ugly, big-eared Heifer, who makes the best sourdough biscuits in the Choctaw county; and beautiful Lucy Washbourne, rebel to the marrow and proud of it. The enemies are men of another breed—hard-bitten Captain Clardy for one, a cruel officer with hatred for Jeff in his eyes and a dark secret on his soul.

Here is a story of a lesser-known part of the Civil War, the Western campaign, different in its issues and its problems, fought with a different savagery. It is a dramatic picture of a war and the men of both sides who fought in it.

100 Cupboards, by Nathan Wilson. Random House, 2006.

When twelve-year-old Henry York comes to stay with his aunt, uncle (who wants to sell tumbleweeds on EBay), and three female cousins in Henry, Kansas, after his parents (who made him ride in a car seat until he was nine) have been kidnapped while bicycling across South America, he has learned from past experience not to look forward to anything. What a surprise when he wakes up one night to find bits of plaster in his hair. Two knobs have broken through the wall above the bed, and one of them is slowly turning.

Henry scrapes the plaster off the wall and discovers cupboards of all different sizes and shapes. Through one he can hear the sound of falling rain. Through another he sees a glowing room—with a man pacing back and forth! Henry soon understands that these are not just cupboards, but portals to other worlds. Before long the dull Kansas landscape is transformed into fantasy journeys.

Steal Away Home, by Lois Ruby. Simon & Schuster, 1999.

Dana's folks have bought an old house in Kansas to fix up as a bed and breakfast. Dana is helping to strip wallpaper when she uncovers a door to a hidden room that contains a skeleton and a diary. The diary belonged to someone who lived in the house before and during the Civil War. The house had been used as a stop on the Underground Railroad, and the skeleton is that of a former slave, Lizbet Charles. The story alternates between the present and 1856 and the efforts of a Quaker family to protect the slaves who used their home as a stopping place and Lizbet Charles, a conductor on the railroad. The puzzle of Lizbet's death is solved in the final chapters as the reader experiences the dangers faced by both the Quaker family and the runaway slaves.

Mystery of the Orphan Train, by Gertrude Chandler Warner. Albert Whitman, 2005.

The Alden family visit an old Kansas inn that's full of secrets! Nobody knows why a famous photographer visited the inn just to take a single picture. And what about the other legendary guest? He was a heroic young stranger who'd come west on an orphan train, the train that came from the East with children who had no families and were hoping to be adopted by people in the small towns where the train stopped. Not to be discouraged when faced with a riddle, the Alden children discover a long lost-riddle that just might solve all these mysteries, if only they can solve it. And, of course, they do.

More Kansas Titles

Dahlberg, Maurine. *Story of Jonas.* Farrar, Straus & Giroux, 2007.

Duey, Kathleen. *Train Wreck Kansas, 1892.* Aladdin, 1999.

Hopkinson, Deborah. *Pioneer Summer.* Simon & Schuster, 2002.

Jennings, Richard. *The Great Whale of Kansas.* Houghton Mifflin, 2001.

Kimmel, Elizabeth. *In the Eye of the Storm.* HarperCollins, 2003.

Kimmel, Elizabeth. *One Sky Above Us.* HarperCollins, 2002.

Kimmel, Elizabeth. *To the Frontier.* HarperCollins, 2002.

Kochenderfer, Lee. *The Victory Garden.* Delacorte, 2001.

McKissack, Pat. *Away West.* Viking, 2006.

McMullen, Kate. *For This Land.* Scholastic, 2003.

Meehl, Brian. *Out of Patience.* Delacorte, 2006.

Moss, Marissa. *Rose's Journal: The Story of a Girl in the Great Depression.* Harcourt, 2001.

Myers, Walter Dean. *Journal of Joshua Loper: Black Cowboy.* Scholastic, 1999.

Nixon, Joan Lowery. *A Dangerous Promise.* Gareth Stevens, 2000.

Nixon, Joan Lowery. *In the Face of Danger.* Gareth Stevens, 2000.

Nixon, Joan Lowery. *Keeping Secrets.* Gareth Stevens, 2000.

Rotkowski, Margaret. *After the Dancing Days.* HarperCollins, 1986.

Seely, Sandra. *Grasslands.* Holiday House, 2002.

Wilson, Nathan. *100 Cupboards.* Random House, 2007.

Kentucky Fact Sheet

Capital: Frankfort

Largest City: Louisville

Entered the Union: June 1, 1792

Tree: Tulip poplar

Flower: Goldenrod

Bird: Kentucky cardinal

Rivers: Ohio, Mississippi, Cumberland, Kentucky, Green

Nickname: Bluegrass State

Products: Agriculture, coal mining

Major Tourist Attractions:
John James Audubon State Park and Museum
Mammoth Cave National Park
Abraham Lincoln's Birthplace National Historic Site
Horse farms near Lexington
The Kentucky Derby is held annually in Louisville

Land Area: 40,400 square miles

Population 2006: 4,117,800

Motto: United We Stand, Divided We Fall

 ## Trivia

- Many of the country's best race horses come from Kentucky.

- The world's largest amount of gold is stored at Fort Knox.

- The famous Kentucky bluegrass was brought to this continent by the colonists.

From *Reading the Fifty States: Booktalks, Response Activities, and More*
by Nancy Polette. Westport, CT: Libraries Unlimited. Copyright © 2009.

Kentucky Booktalks

Gabriel's Horses, by Alison Hart. Peachtree, 2007.

The year is 1864, and twelve-year-old Gabriel hopes to one day become a famous jockey. Although he is the son of a free black father and a slave mother, making him a slave as well, he loves to help his father, one of the best horse trainers in Kentucky, care for the racehorses on Master Giles's farm.

But the violence of war disrupts the familiar routine of daily life on the farm. One-Arm Dan Parmer and his band of Confederate raiders are threatening area farms and stealing horses. When Gabriel's father enlists in a Colored Battalion to help the Union Army and raise enough money to purchase freedom for his wife and son, Gabriel is both proud and worried. But the absence of his father brings the arrival of Mr. Newcastle, a white horse trainer with harsh, cruel methods for handling horses and people. Now it is up to Gabriel to protect the horses he loves from Mr. Newcastle and keep them safely out of the clutches of One-Arm Dan and his men.

Gabriel's Journey, by Alison Hart. Peachtree, 2008.

Ex-slave Gabriel leaves behind a successful horse racing career to join his parents at Camp Nelson, where his father is a sergeant in the fifth U.S. Colored Cavalry of the Union Army. Twelve-year-old Gabriel is too young to join the regiment as a soldier, but he finds a job as a personal groom to Champion, the unruly horse that belongs to Colonel Waite, the white commander. When the cavalry receives orders to join white regiments in an attack on the Virginia salt works, Gabriel surreptitiously gets hold of a horse and uniform and joins the troops. But being a soldier is a lot harder than he imagined. Bad weather, rough riding, dwindling supplies, and blatant racism wear heavily on his spirit. When his father and Colonel Waite are not among the weary and wounded men who return from battle, Gabriel mounts Champion and rides to the battlefield in search of them. This is a gripping story that brings to life the danger and drama of a time when war and issues of race and freedom divided the country.

Borrowed Children, by George Ella Lyon. University of Kentucky Press, 1999.

Mandy Perritt is a character readers will long remember. The twelve-year-old loves school and is more than upset when she has to leave school to care for her family of eight. Mandy's mother has given birth to brother William and must remain in bed for at least six weeks. The chores of cleaning, cooking, and taking care of a new baby are carried out in a farmhouse with no electricity and no running water. Understandably, Mandy is angry and upset. She would like to be anywhere other than Gooserock, Kentucky, and feels the burden placed on her is most unfair.

Mother does get better, and as a reward for all her hard work, Mandy's parents send her at Christmas time to Memphis on a visit with her grandparents. There she learns about her mother's childhood and about family members she knew little about. Best of all, Many learns to understand and appreciate each member of her large family.

The Keeper of the Doves, by Betsy Byars. Viking, 2002.

Amen McBee, the youngest of five sisters, gobbles up words the way other children gobble up sweets. She wrote her first poem at the age of six. She couldn't be more different from her elder twin sisters Arabella and Annabella, called the Bellas. Amen's mother is frequently unwell, and the care and discipline of the children is done by Aunt Pauline. The twins constantly frighten Amen with stories about Mr. Tominski, the old recluse, the keeper of the doves, who lives in their chapel. The twins insist that Mr. Tominski is a dangerous bogeyman who eats children whole, but Papa vows that the old man wouldn't hurt a soul. In addition to Papa, Mother, and the ever-scolding Aunt Pauline, the reader will meet a loving grandmother who brings cameras for everyone. When tragedy involving the keeper of the doves strikes the family, Amen commemorates his place in the family with a poem. Papa was right: the keeper of the doves was not a monster.

More Kentucky Titles

Ayres, Katherine. *Stealing South: A Story of the Underground Railroad.* Delacorte, 2001.

Birdseye, Tom. *A Tough Nut to Crack.* Holiday House, 2007.

Dadey, Debbie. *Whistler's Hollow.* Bloomsbury Children's Books, 2002.

Hart, Alison. *Danger at the Wild West Show.* Pleasant Company, 2003.

Hemphill, Helen. *Runaround.* Front Street, 2007.

Keehn, Sally M. *Magpie Gabbard and the Quest for the Buried Moon.* Philomel, 2007.

Ketchum, Liza *Orphan Journey Home.* Avon Books, 2000.

Meltzer, Milton. *Underground Man.* Harcourt, 1972. Reissued 2006.

Mitchell, Elizabet. *Journey to the Bottomless Pit.* Viking, 2004.

Pearsall, Shelley. *Trouble Don't Last.* Dell Yearling, 2003.

Platt, Chris. *Willow King: Race the Wind.* Random House, 2000.

Pryor, Bonnie. *Joseph, a Rumble of War, 1861.* Morrow, 1999.

Pryor, Bonnie. *Joseph's Choice, 1861.* HarperCollins, 2000.

Rinaldi, Ann. *The Coffin Quilt: The Feud Between the Hatfields and the McCoys.* Harcourt, 1999.

Skinner, Constance Lindsay. *Becky Landers: Frontier Warrior.* Bethlehem Books, 2006.

Steele, William Owen. *Year of the Bloody Sevens.* Harcourt, 1963.

White, Ruth. *Tadpole.* Dell Yearling, 2004.

Woodson, Jacqueline. *Lena.* Delacorte Press, 1999.

Wyeth, Sharon Dennis. *Flying Free.* Scholastic, 2000.

Louisiana Fact Sheet

Capital: Baton Rouge

Largest City: New Orleans

Entered the Union: April 30, 1812

Tree: Bald cypress

Flower: Magnolia

Bird: Eastern brown pelican

Rivers: Atchafalay, Mississippi, Red

Nickname: Pelican State

Products: Cotton, oil, natural gas, salt

Major Tourist Attractions:
New Orleans
The Bayou region
The Gulf of Mexico coastline

Land Area: 51,840 square miles

Population 2006: 4,500,000

Motto: Union, Justice and Confidence

Trivia

- Louisiana leads all other states in the production of salt.

- The Mardi Gras celebration has been held in New Orleans since 1838.

- Gueydan, Louisiana, is the duck capital of America.

- The famous Battle of New Orleans was fought two weeks after the War of 1812 ended.

Louisiana Booktalks

Sugarcane Academy, by Michael Tisserand. Harcourt, 2007.

This is the true story of how a New Orleans teacher and his storm-struck students created a school to remember. Because Hurricane Katrina struck at the beginning of the school year, the children of New Orleans were among those most affected. Michael Tisserand evacuated his family to New Iberia, Louisiana, where one of his children's teachers, Paul Reynaud, was living as well. Tisserand and other parents persuaded Reynaud to start a school among the sugar cane fields.

So was born the Sugarcane Academy, as the children themselves named it, and so also began an experience none of Reynaud's pupils will ever forget. This inspiring book shows how a dedicated teacher made the best out of the worst situation, and how the children of New Orleans, of all backgrounds and races, were affected by Katrina but learned to live with its consequences.

My Louisiana Sky, by Kimberly Willis Holt. Random House, 2000.

Tiger Ann Parker finds that there is more than one kind of prejudice. She is a bright twelve-year-old and a talented baseball player, but neither is enough for her to be accepted by the other girls in her class. Their taunts about her parents hurt because both parents are mentally disabled. Her father can't read an electric bill, and her mother's childish behavior is often embarrassing. Tiger's Grandmother runs the house, and as Tiger says, "She has enough brains for all of us."

All this changes with Grandmother's sudden death. Tiger's Aunt Dorie Kay offers the girl a home in Baton Rouge, where she can live a normal life not burdened by her parents' disabilities. But Tiger knows if she accepts her aunt's offer, she will break her parents' hearts. Should she head to Baton Rouge for a better, freer life with her aunt, or take on the responsibility of caring for her parents? The sudden revelation of a dark family secret prompts Tiger to make a decision that will ultimately change her life.

Dust from Old Bones, by Sandra Forrester. HarperCollins, 1999.

In 1838 New Orleans we find Simone Racine and her family, all of mixed race. The story is told by Simone in diary form and covers a four-month period from April to July. In her diary entries we learn abut Simone's wish to be more like her light-skinned cousin Claire-Marie. We meet Claire-Marie's father, who abandons Claire-Marie and his family with no support; Tante Maria, who helps one niece while betraying another; Tante Madelon, who arrives from Paris to visit Simone's dying Grandfather; the dark family secrets Grandfather's death reveals; and last of all Simone's decision to put her courage to the test in helping her aunt's slaves to escape. This is an engrossing tale of a courageous young woman.

Mister and Me, by Kimberly Holt. Putnam, 1999.

Jolene is an African American child who faces all the trappings of racism and prejudice in her small Louisiana town in 1940. Colored people must sit in the back part of the balcony at the movie theater. There are no movies starring African Americans, but that is to be expected. Jolene knows she must speak politely to Miz Logan, the Mill owner's wife, if Jolene's mother wants to continue to be her sewing lady.

Life at home, however, is different. The Johnson home s filled with love, with only one slight problem. Leroy Redfield, a logger, comes courting Jolene's mother. He is a good man, but Jolene does everything in her power to discourage the romance. She even cuts to pieces some expensive material he brought Jolene's mother as a gift. As time passes, Jolene finds her resentment is unfounded, and she comes to accept her mother's marriage to Leroy. In accepting Leroy she also accepts the uncertainties of her own future.

More Louisiana Titles

Buckey, Sarah Masters. *The Smuggler's Treasure.* Pleasant Company, 1999.

Couvillon, Jacques. *The Chicken Dance.* Bloomsbury, 2007.

Doucet, Sharon Arms. *Fiddle Fever.* Clarion Books, 2000.

Duncan, Lois. *Locked in Time.* Dell, 1991.

Gutman, Dan. *The Million Dollar Shot.* Hyperion, 2003.

Holt, Kimberly Willis. *Part of Me: Stories of a Louisiana Family.* Holt, 2006.

LaFaye, A. *The Strength of Saints.* Simon & Schuster, 2002.

Lane, Dakota. *Johnny Voodoo.* Random House, 1997.

Marcum, Lance. *The Cottonmouth Club.* Farrar, Straus & Giroux, 2005.

McBride, Roger. *On the Banks of the Bayou.* HarperCollins, 1998.

Molloy, Michael. *Peter Raven Under Fire.* Scholastic, 2005.

Nixon, Joan Lowery. *The Haunting.* Delacorte, 1998.

Shaik, Fatima. *Melitte.* Dial, 1997.

Siegelson, Kim. *Honey Bea.* Hyperion, 2006.

Tedrow, Thomas. *The World's Fair.* Thomas Nelson, 1992.

Walter, Mildred Pitts. *Ray and the Best Family Reunion Ever.* HarperCollins, 2002.

Woods, Brenda. *The Red Rose Box.* Putnam, 2002.

Maine Fact Sheet

Capital: Augusta

Largest City: Portland

Entered the Union: March 15, 1820

Tree: White pine

Flower: White pine cone and tassel

Bird: Chickadee

Rivers: Androscoggin, Kennebec, Penobscot

Nickname: Pine Tree State

Products: Wood products, paper, seafood

Major Tourist Attractions:
Cadillac Mountain in Acadia National Park
Baxter State Park
Kennebunkport, the summer home of George Bush Sr.
West Quoddy Head, the easternmost point in the U.S.

Land Area: 35,385 square miles

Population 2006: 1,305,728

Motto: I Direct

 ## Trivia

- Maine lobster is world famous; 40 million pounds are caught every year.

- Maine is the world's largest grower and supplier of blueberries.

- Maine workers make 100 million toothpicks a day.

From *Reading the Fifty States: Booktalks, Response Activities, and More* by Nancy Polette. Westport, CT: Libraries Unlimited. Copyright © 2009.

Maine Booktalks

Sign of the Beaver, by Elizabeth George Speare. Houghton Mifflin, 1983.

Twelve-year-old Matt shook his head in disgust. The disgust was with himself. It was his carelessness that let the stranger in the house . . . the stranger who took off in the night with Matt's gun, his only means of getting food. It was his carelessness that left the cabin open to a hungry bear, who destroyed everything in sight and took the little food Matt had left.

When Matt's father left to get the rest of the family, he trusted Matt to care for himself for the few weeks he would be alone. And Matt had let him down. Fish was still plentiful, and he had his hook and line. It looked like a steady diet of fish was ahead. Then Matt remembered . . . the bee tree! A taste of honey sure would be a treat.

It was an easy tree to climb, and the bees didn't even seem to notice as he pulled himself higher and higher. Peering in a small hole, he could just glimpse far inside the golden mass of honeycomb. The bark around the hole was rotted and crumbling. He put his fingers on the edge and gave a slight tug. A good-sized piece of bark broke off in his hand.

With it came the bees. The humming grew to a roar, like a great wind. Matt felt a sharp pain, and another and another. The angry creatures swarmed along his hands and bare arms, in his hair, on his face.

Matt's only hope was to make it to the icy cold water of the river. This was the most careless thing he had ever done, and he'd live to regret it . . . if, that is, he lived.

Calico Bush, by Rachel Field. Simon & Schuster, 1998.

Marguerite LeDoux is a young French immigrant forced to work as a servant to the Sargent family after losing her family. She must go with the family as they move to a deserted stretch of land filled with danger and threatened by Indians along the sparsely inhabited Maine coast. In one year's time Marguerite lives through both failure and success in a strange land as she adapts to the trials of pioneer life.

The Ghost of Lizard Light, by Elvira Woodruff. Sagebrush Books, 2001.

When you are in the fourth grade and have a best friend named Denton and a pet lizard, life deals you a blow when your parents decide to move. To make matters worse, the move is from Iowa to Maine. Jack Carlton finds himself in this situation, with nothing he can do about it. His father is a school principal (who gives him math problems to work on during the summer) and his mother is a costume designer who flits around the house in weird costumes; his little sister, Franny, plans to be a vet and practices with bandages on everything she touches.

Some of Jack's unhappiness with the move is eased, however, when he finds an old lighthouse on the property. As Jack explores, he meets Nathaniel Witherspoon, a ghost. Nathaniel and his father had been lighthouse keepers, but Nathaniel's death was not recorded correctly in history. Nathaniel wants Jack to set the record straight. The boys become good friends as the reader experiences a supernatural seafaring adventure and Jack is able to fulfill Nathaniel's request.

Mystery Isle, by Judith St. George. Puffin Books, 2007.

Bright, curious thirteen-year-old Kim is not looking forward to a summer on Shag Island in rural Maine. The island and the mansion on it have been in her family for generations, but now Kim's great-grandfather intends to sell both. Kim and her mother busy themselves with preparations, but when her mother is called away on business, Kim and Great Grandpa find themselves alone on the island. Strange music, flashing lights, and an odd parrot suddenly hunt them, and Great Grandpa is convinced he is losing his mind. But Kim knows what she saw, and as she digs into the mystery, she soon realizes they are in grave danger. Now she must discover what or who is haunting Shag Island. Their lives depend on it.

More Maine Titles

Bellairs, John. *The Chessmen of Doom.* Dial, 1989.

Blume, Judy. *Fudge-a-Mania.* Dutton, 1990.

Bradley, Kimberly. *Halfway to the Sky.* Delacorte, 2002.

Carey, Janet. *Molly's Fire.* Atheneum, 2000.

Copeland, Cynthia. *Elin's Island.* Millbrook Press, 2003.

Deans, Sis. *Rainy.* Holt, 2005.

Garden, Nancy. *Meeting Melanie.* Farrar, Straus & Giroux, 2002.

Gutman, Dan. *The Get Rich Quick Club.* HarperCollins, 2004.

Hopkinson, Deborah. *Birdie's Lighthouse.* Atheneum, 1997.

Howland, Ethan. *The Lobster War.* Front Street Books, 2001.

Jones, Kimberly. *Sand Dollar Summer.* Atheneum, 2006.

Kinsey-Warner, Natalie. *Gifts from the Sea.* Random House, 2003.

Levin, Betty. *Shadow Catcher.* Greenwillow, 2000.

Roy, Ron. *The White Wolf.* Random House, 2004.

Schmidt, Gary. *Lizzie Bright and the Buckminster Boy.* Clarion, 2004.

Scoppettone, Sandra. *Playing Murder.* HarperCollins, 1985.

Wait, Lea. *Finest Kind.* Atheneum, 2006.

Wait, Lee. *Wintering Well.* Atheneum, 2004.

Wallace-Brodeur, Ruth. *Heron Cove.* Dutton, 2005.

Maryland Fact Sheet

Capital: Annapolis

Largest City: Baltimore

Entered the Union: April 28, 1788

Tree: White oak

Flower: Black-eyed Susan

Bird: Baltimore oriole

Rivers: Patapsco, Patuxent, Potomac, Susquehanna

Nicknames: Free State and Old Line State

Products: Agriculture, poultry and dairy products, coal, seafood

Major Tourist Attractions:
    U.S. Naval Academy, Annapolis
    Baltimore Inner Harbor
    Antietam National Battlefield near Sharpsburg

Land Area: 12,407 square miles

Population 2006: 5,508,900

Motto: Manly Deeds, Womanly Words

 ## Trivia

- Largest employer is the federal government.

- Most of Maryland's people live on the Western Shore.

- "The Star Spangled Banner" was written during the bombardment of Fort McHenry durig the War of 1812.

- Annapolis is America's sailing capital.

Maryland Booktalks

Stealing Freedom, by Elisa Carbone. Random House, 2001.

Ann Maria is twelve. Her father is a free man, but Ann Maria, her mother, and her brothers and sisters are slaves. They are owned by the Prices and work in their inn and on their farm. The family worries about being split apart when Mr. Price begins selling slaves to raise money to pay his gambling debts.

Both of Ann Maria's brothers are sold. The Vigilance Committee helps Ann Maria's father buy freedom for his wife and daughter, Catherine. The Prices, however, refuse to let Ann go. Mrs. Price is a cruel mistress, and Ann Maria is sad and discouraged, sure that she will always be a slave. The one bright light in her life is Alfred, a slave on a neighboring plantation. She promises she won't run away without him, but then she is whisked away by the abolitionists and begins her journey to Canada and freedom on the Underground Railroad, facing with courage the uncertainties and dangers that lie ahead.

A Thief on Morgan's Plantation, by Lisa Banim. Silver Moon Press, 2000.

In 1861 the United States was on the brink of a Civil War. Northern and Southern states disagreed on many issues, a major issue being slavery. Come visit Morgan's Plantation and see firsthand what it was like to be the son or daughter of the plantation owner and what it was like to be the son or daughter of a slave. When her father heads west to look for gold, Constance is sent to live with her cousins on Morgan's Plantation, just outside of Baltimore. Soon after her arrival the eleven-year-old finds that her uncle's watch has been stolen. Ezra, a young slave has been accused of the crime, but Constance and her cousin, Toby, don't believe Ezra is guilty. They set out to find the real thief. Before the mystery is solved the reader will hear both sides of the slavery issue and see Constance interact with both kind and obnoxious characters.

The Jellyfish Season, by Mary Downing Hahn. HarperCollins, 1992.

Kathleen Foster is twelve. Her father is out of work. He and many others have been laid off from the steel plant, so he must remain in Baltimore to look for a job. Meanwhile Kathleen, her three younger sisters, and her mother travel to a Chesapeake Bay resort community to stay with relatives. The intrusion of the Foster family is highly resented by cousin Fay. Fay is fourteen but has told a twenty-year-old boyfriend she met on the beach; she told him that she is eighteen. When the Foster girls see Fay' s boyfriend at the beach, Fay swears them to secrecy, but Patsy reveals Fay's secret in the middle of an argument. Not only is the romance broken up, but during the argument Kathleen hears truths about her family that confirm her fears about her parents. This is a well-told story about a young teen who faces problems that at first seem too difficult to solve.

Retreat from Gettysburg, by Kathleen Ernst. White Mane Books, 2000.

It is 1863, two years into the bloody Civil War. Chigger O'Malley has lost his father and three brothers to the fighting. He is both sad and vengeful and wants to join the Union Army to kill the Confederates who killed his father and brother. Chigger, however, does not want to leave his mother alone in their Maryland home. Then a Southern army in full retreat from the terrible Battle of Gettysburg leaves a wounded officer in the care of Chiggar's mother. Chiggar's first thought is murder, but the officer, Captain Tallard, is a kind and humane man whom Chiggar eventually comes to respect. When the Union army draws near, Chiggar is determined to save Captain Tallard and to see that he gets back home.

Here is a war novel in which the two sides are not sharply defined. Are those who fight in wars bad people? Or are many good people caught up in bad circumstances?

More Maryland Titles

Cummings, Priscilla. *A Face First.* Dutton, 2001.

Curtis, Alice. *A Little Maid of Maryland.* Applewood, 1996.

Hahn, Mary Downing. *Anna on the Farm.* Clarion, 2001.

Hahn, Mary Downing. *Promises to the Dead.* Clarion, 2000.

Jackson, Dave. *Listen for the Whippoorwill.* Bethany House, 1993.

Kimball, K. M. *Star Spangled Secret.* Tandem, 2001.

McCully, Emily. *The Battle for St. Michael's.* HarperCollins, 2002.

Mills, Claudia. *The Totally Made-Up Civil War Diary of Amanda MacLeish.* Farrar, Straus & Giroux, 2008.

Naylor, Phyllis Reynolds. *Lovingly Alice.* Atheneum, 2004.

Naylor, Phyllis Reynolds. *Starting with Alice.* Atheneum, 2002.

Paterson, Katherine. *Jacob Have I Loved.* HarperCollins, 1990.

Reeder, Carolyn. *Before the Creeks Ran Red.* HarperCollins, 2003.

Reeder, Carolyn. *Captain Kate.* Avon Books, 1999.

Rinaldi, Ann. *Amelia's War.* Scholastic, 1999.

Rodowsky, Colby. *Not Quite a Stranger.* Farrar, Straus & Giroux, 2003.

Scillian, Devin. *Pappy's Handkerchief.* Sleeping Bear Press, 2007.

Troeger, Virginia. *Secret Along the St. Mary's.* Silver Moon Press, 2003.

Weinberg, Karen. *Window of Time.* White Mane, 1991.

Massachusetts Fact Sheet

Capital: Boston

Largest City: Boston

Entered the Union: February 6, 1788

Tree: American elm

Flower: Mayflower

Bird: Chickadee

Rivers: Charles, Merrimack, Connecticut

Nicknames: Bay State and Old Colony State

Products: Textiles, computers, printed materials

Major Tourist Attractions:
The Freedom Trail in Boston
Plimoth Plantation; Nantucket Island
Basketball Hall of Fame in Springfield

Land Area: 10,555 square miles

Population 2006: 6,430,400

Motto: We Seek Peace but Peace Only Under Liberty

 ## Trivia

- Harvard University, in Boston, is the first college established in the Americas.

- The first World Series was played in Boston in 1903.

- Home of the first U.S. lighthouse.

From *Reading the Fifty States: Booktalks, Response Activities, and More* by Nancy Polette. Westport, CT: Libraries Unlimited. Copyright © 2009.

Massachusetts Booktalks

Lyddie, by Katherine Paterson. Dutton, 1991.

She was no better than a slave, Lyddie thought The debt-ridden farm had been let to a neighbor, and she and her brother had been hired out. Was the end really near, as their mother had said when she fled with the babies after the hungry bear had broken into their Vermont farm house? That winter of 1843, the two children had been left to fend for themselves. If only their long-gone father would return and set things right.

It is the promise of a new and better life that finally prompts Lyddie to journey to the mill town of Lowell, Massachusetts. As a factory girl, she will earn a wage and be free. No matter that she has to live in a crowded boarding house, that the clatter of incessant looms is deafening, and that the murky, lint-filled air brings on fevers and wracking coughs. Despite the menacing overseer, Lyddie works long, exhausting hours to be able to pay off the debt and regain her beloved farm. But does she jeopardize her job and her family's future by being friends with the radical Diana and perhaps signing a petition for better conditions? Indomitable Lyddie grows in mind and spirit in this novel about social change.

Johnny Tremain, by Esther Forbes. Houghton Mifflin, 1943.

Clever and gifted Johnny Tremain is apprenticed to a silversmith in the year 1773. Johnny sees a great future ahead, until the day that carelessness causes his hand to be so badly burned that his dreams of being a silversmith are gone. Johnny becomes bitter and feels useless, until he becomes a dispatch rider for the Committee of Public Safety and gets to know the men who will be the leaders of the revolution. With the rapid events that follow leading to independence, Johnny fills a valuable role in securing the nation's freedom from English oppression. Live through two years of history with Johnny Tremain and watch through his eyes as the American Revolution unfolds.

Finding Providence, by Avi. HarperCollins, 1997.

Told by his daughter, Mary, this is the true account of the expulsion of Roger Williams from the Massachusetts Bay Colony in 1635. He is put on trial for preaching ideas such as that magistrates should not be allowed to interfere with religious teaching and that there should be freedom of religion for all people. After lengthy questioning by John Cotton, Williams is expelled from the Colony. As he departs he tells his family that they must trust in God's providence to see him to safety. In his travels Williams becomes friends with the Narragansett Indians, from whom he purchases land that will become Providence, Rhode Island, where all are welcome to worship as they wish.

Amos Fortune Free Man, by Elizabeth Yates. Dutton, 1950.

At-Mun was a prince, the son of an African king. As a young boy of fifteen he was stolen from his home by slave traders, endured the inhuman ocean crossing on a slave ship, and was sold in America to a Quaker named Copeland. The Copeland family lived in Boston and immediately gave At-Mun a new name, Amos Fortune. Fortune was in some ways an appropriate name, because Amos was treated better by the family he served than were most slaves. The Copeland family taught Amos to read and write. Mr. Copeland died before freeing Amos, but Amos was finally able to become a free man. He then devoted his life to helping others gain their freedom.

More Massachusetts Titles

Alter, Stephen. *The Phantom Isles.* Bloomsbury, 2007.

Buchanan, Jane. *Goodbye Charley.* Farrar, Straus & Giroux, 2004.

Dennenberg, Barry. *Mirror, Mirror on the Wall.* Scholastic, 2002.

Duble, Katherine. *The Sacrifice.* Atheneum, 2005.

Duey, Khlen. *Silence and Lily: 1773.* Dutton, 2007.

Fraustino, Lisa. *I Walk in Dread.* Scholastic, 2004.

Harlow, Joan. *Midnight Rider.* Atheneum, 2005.

Hermes, Parricia. *Salem Witch.* Kingfisher, 2006.

Hurst, Carol Otis. *In Plain Sight.* Houghton Mifflin, 2002.

Hurst, Carol Otis. *Torchlight.* Houghton Mifflin, 2006.

Hurst, Carol Otis. *The Wrong One.* Houghton Mifflin, 2003.

Hurst, Carol Otis. *You Come to Yokum.* Houghton Mifflin, 2002.

Karr, Kathleen. *Gilbert and Sullivan Set Me Free.* Hyperion, 2003.

Kirwan, Anna. *Of Flowers and Shadows.* Scholastic, 2005.

Langton, Jane. *The Mysterious Circus.* HarperCollins, 2005.

Lewis , Maggie. *Morgy Coast to Coast.* Houghton Mifflin, 2005.

Paterson, Katherine. *Bread and Roses, Too.* Clarion, 2006.

Roy, Ron. *Mayflower Treasure Hunt.* Random House, 2007.

Turner, Ann. *Love Thy Neighbor.* Scholastic, 2003.

Wallace-Brodeur, Ruth, *Blue Eyes Better.* Dutton, 2002.

White, Ellen. *Where Have All the Flowers Gone?* Scholastic, 2002.

Michigan Fact Sheet

Capital: Lansing

Largest City: Detroit

Entered the Union: January 26, 1837

Tree: White pine

Flower: Apple blossom

Bird: Robin

Rivers: Detroit, Kalamazoo, Grand, St. Mary's, St. Clair

Nickname: Wolverine State

Products: Agriculture, automobiles, lumber

Major Tourist Attractions:
Pictured Rocks National Lakeshore
Mackinac Island
Soo Canals

Land Area: 96,810 square miles

Population 2006: 10,000,985

Motto: If You Seek a Pleasant Peninsula, Look About You

Trivia

- Most of Michigan's people live in the lower peninsula.

- The French were the first to settle Michigan.

- More breakfast cereal is made in Battle Creek than in any other place in the world.

Michigan Booktalks

Bud, Not Buddy, by Christopher Paul Curtis. Delacorte Press, 1999.

In 1936 in Flint, Michigan, times were hard, and Bud is a homeless boy on the run. Mistreated in a foster home, he runs away, taking only his precious suitcase with a picture of the father he hopes to find The picture is on a flyer advertising Herman Calloway and the Dusky Devastators. He hitchhikes to Grand Rapids, where the band is supposed to be, receiving help on the way from Mr. Lewis, who sends a telegram to Herman Calloway telling him when the boy will arrive. Bud does reach Grand Rapids and the place where the band is playing. Herman, who is up in years, wants nothing to do with the boy, who is taken under the wing of the band's lead singer. When the contents of Bud's suitcase are finally revealed, Bud discovers that Herman is his grandfather and with the help of other members of the band, can look forward to a brighter future.

Willow Run, by Patricia Reilly Giff. Random House, 2007.

Early in World War II workers were flocking to Willow Run, Michigan, to work in the factories turning out war planes. Meggie's father was one of these workers, who moved his family to Willow Run from Rockaway, New York. Meggie worries about her German-born grandfather, left behind in Rockaway. Even though he is a loyal American, he may well suffer because of where he was born. She worries, too, about her brother, Eddie, fighting overseas and reported missing in action. Meggie misses her New York home and friends but meets other kids who have left their home states as well. At one point in the story Meggie steals money from an ice cream seller, thinking the seller is a spy. She eventually learns that courage must come from within and that keeping hope alive is important for both oneself and others.

Hannah, by Gloria Whelan. Random House, 1993.

In 1887 a blind child had little hope of getting an education. Parents protected their blind children by keeping them sheltered in the confines of their home. This is the situation for nine-year-old Hannah, who longs to go to school like the other children of the town but is kept safe at home by her parents. After all, what kind of education could a child receive who could not see? Things change when a free-spirited teacher, Lydia Robbin, arrives to live with the family. She sees not only Hannah's intelligence but her creativity and convinces Hannah's mother to send her to school. The first day is filled with challenges and is less than successful, but little by little Hannah overcomes each obstacle to prove to her fellow students and her parents that she can learn. In the end her fellow students band together to earn the money to purchase a Braille writer, and the class bully has a change of heart.

Indian School, by Gloria Whelan. HarperCollins, 1997.

The year is 1839, and eleven-year-old Lucy has lost both parents in a wagon accident. She is sent to live with the Wilkinses, her Aunt Emma and Uncle Edward, who run an Indian school in Northern Michigan. Aunt Emma is overly strict with her charges and refuses to take in two children who have survived a smallpox epidemic. Uncle Edward insists that the children be cared for, and Aunt Emma reluctantly accepts the children but treats both harshly. The girl, Raven, rebels against the strict discipline and runs away. Lucy, who has become friends with Raven, feels her aunt has been not only harsh but cruel in trying to separate Raven and her brother. She knows the time has come to stand up for what is right.

More Michigan Titles

Curtis, Rebecca. *Charlotte Avery on Isle Royale.* Midwest Traditions, 1995.

Fenner, Carol. *Yolanda's Genius.* Simon & Schuster, 1995.

Forman, James. *Becca's Story.* Scribner, 1992.

Goodman, Susan. *Robert Henry Hendershot.* Aladdin, 2003.

Hall, Lynn. *Dragon Defiant.* Follett, 1977.

Lowery, Linda. *Truth and Salsa.* Peachtree, 2006.

Martin, C. L. *Day of Darkness, Night of Light.* Dillon Press, 1898.

Martin, Terri. *A Family Trait.* Holiday House, 1999.

Rinaldi, Ann. *Girl in Blue.* Scholastic, 2007.

Stahl, Hilda T. *The White Pine Chronicles.* Thomas Nelson, 1993.

Trotter, Maxine. *Sister to the Wolf.* Kids Can Press, 2004.

Warner, Gertrude Chandler. *Mystery in the Old Attic.* Whitman, 1997.

Whelan, Gloria. *Night of the Full Moon.* Knopf, 1993.

Whelan, Gloria. *Shadow of the Wolf.* Random House, 1999.

Whelan, Gloria. *The Wanigan.* Knopf, 2002.

White, Ruth. *Memories of Summer.* Farrar, Straus & Giroux, 2000.

Minnesota Fact Sheet

Capital: St. Paul

Largest City: Minneapolis

Entered the Union: May 11, 1858

Tree: Red pine

Flower: Lady slipper

Bird: Common loon

Rivers: Minnesota, Mississippi, Rainy, Red

Nicknames: North Star State, Gopher State, Land of 10,000 Lakes

Products: Agriculture, dairy products, iron ore

Major Tourist Attractions:
Boundary Waters Canoe Area
Lake Itaska
St. Paul Winter Carnival

Land Area: 86,943 square miles

Population 2006: 5,060,375

Motto: The Star of the North

 ## Trivia

- The Mississippi River divides the twin cities of St. Paul and Minneapolis.

- Minnesota has more than 15,000 lakes.

- Anoka, Minnesota, is the Halloween capital of the world.

From *Reading the Fifty States: Booktalks, Response Activities, and More* by Nancy Polette. Westport, CT: Libraries Unlimited. Copyright © 2009.

Minnesota Booktalks

The Shrouding Woman, by Loretta Ellsworth. Holt, 2002.

When eleven-year-old Evie's mother dies, her father asks his sister, Aunt Flo, to come and care for Evie and her younger sister, Mae. The time is right after the Civil War and the place is Crooked Creek Valley in southeastern Minnesota. Aunt Flo is almost the opposite of Evie's mother, and to make matters worse, she is a shrouding woman, a woman who prepares bodies for burial. Evie wants nothing to do with even the idea of death and is both fascinated and repelled by the brown box Aunt Flo keeps under her bed containing the tools of her trade. Because the role of a shrouding woman is usually passed from mother to daughter, Evie fears that Aunt Flo might one day expect her to take over the task, especially when Aunt Flo asks the girl to help lay out a young woman who has died in childbirth. Eventually Aunt Flo gains Evie's trust, as the girl's stubborn nature softens with the understanding that death is part of life and that Aunt Flo helps to ease the suffering of the living.

The Journal of Otto Peltonen, a Finnish Immigrant, by William Durbin. Scholastic, 2000.

Otto is a fifteen-year-old Finnish boy. His father had left Finland a year earlier to go to the United States and work in the iron mines on the Mesabi Range in Minnesota. At last father saves enough money to send for the family, Otto, his mother, and two sisters. The land of opportunity, however, turns out to be one of grim existence, including an ugly shack, treacherous conditions in the mines, and greedy mine owners who won't listen to the workers. Because both Otto and his father are wood carvers, they are able to save money toward buying the farm the family wants. In the meantime Otto's father is not afraid to fight for the union that the mistreated miners so desperately need.

The Rising Star of Rusty Nail, by Lesley M. M. Blume. Knopf/Random House, 2007.

In 1953 Franny is ten. She lives in an apartment with her family in Rusty Nail, Minnesota, a sleepy little town with no claim to fame. Franny, however, is a gifted pianist and has a great opportunity to develop her talent when Olga Malenkov, a famous Russian concert pianist arrives in Rusty Nail. Franny convinces the woman to teach her in exchange for cleaning her house. Other people of the town are less than friendly to Olga, but under her teaching Franny's skill as a pianist grows. The one thorn in Franny's side is the wealthy and stuck-up Nancy Orilee. Franny is crushed when Nancy's father bribes the judges in a statewide piano contest, and Nancy wins the prize. Then Franny discovers that winning a prize may not be the most important thing after all.

On the Banks of Plum Creek, by Laura Ingalls Wilder. HarperCollins, 1981.

The little house on the prairie is left behind as the Ingalls family sets up housekeeping in a sod house on the banks of Plum Creek in Minnesota. The earthen dugout is not as primitive as it seems, however, for Pa has built it with real glass windows and a hinged door. Laura, the heroine of the tale, is a spunky eight-year-old. She and her sister, Mary, do daily chores together, go to school, and catch fish in the creek. In the evening Pa brings the house alive with fiddle music. The family survives a plague of locusts, a prairie fire, and a blizzard and meets each new challenge determined to win no matter what nature may have in store for them.

More Minnesota Titles

Bauer, Marion Dane. *A Bear Named Trouble.* Clarion, 2005.

Bauer, Marion Dane. *Land of Buffalo Bones.* Scholastic, 2003.

Brown, Jackie. *Little Cricket.* Hyperion, 2004.

Casanova, Mary. *Dog-napped.* Aladdin, 2006.

Casanova, Mary. *When Eagles Fall.* Hyperion, 2002.

Gray, Dianne. *Tomorrow the River.* Houghton Mifflin, 2006.

Haynes, Davie. *The Gumma Wars.* Milkweed, 1997.

Helgerson, Joseph. *Horns and Wrinkles.* Houghton Mifflin, 2006.

Johnson, Lois. *Midnight Rescue.* Bethany House, 1996.

Paulsen, Gary. *The Quilt.* Wendy Lamb Books, 2004.

Rylant, Cynthia. *Old Town in the Green Groves.* HarperCollins, 2002.

Schultz, Jan. *Battle Cry.* Carolrhoda, 2006.

Schultz, Jan. *Horse Sense.* Carolrhoda, 2001.

Shaw, Janet. *Kirsten and the Chippewa.* Pleasant Company, 2002.

Shaw, Janet. *Kirsten's Promise.* Pleasant Company, 2003.

Sommerdorf, Norma. *Red River Girl.* Holiday House, 2006.

Weaver, Will. *Claws.* HarperCollins, 2003.

Weaver, Will. *Full Service.* Farrar, Straus & Giroux, 2005.

Ylvisaka, Anne. *Dear Papa.* Candlewick, 2002.

Mississippi Fact Sheet

Capital: Jackson

Largest City: Jackson

Entered the Union: December 10, 1817

Tree: Magnolia

Flower: Magnolia

Bird: Mockingbird

Rivers: Big Black, Mississippi, Pearl Yazoo

Nickname: Magnolia State

Products: Cotton, textiles, petroleum refining

Major Tourist Attractions:
Old Capitol Building Museum
Delta Queen steamboat
Mansions of Natchez
Gulf Port of Biloxi

Land Area: 48,430 square miles

Population 2006: 10,095,643

Motto: By Valor and Arms

Trivia

- The French were the first to establish a colony in Mississippi, in 1699.

- Root beer was invented in Biloxi in 1898.

Mississippi Booktalks

The Gold Cadillac, by Mildred Taylor. Dial, 1987.

Lois and Wilma, sisters, are thrilled when their father trades in the family car for a shiny gold Cadillac. Even the seats are a shiny gold, and the girls can't wait to be taken for a ride through Toledo, where they live. Father obliges, but Mother-dear refuses to ride in the car. The year is 1950, and according to Mother-dear, the money spent for the gold Cadillac should have been saved to put toward buying a house. Father decides to drive the car to Mississippi to visit the children's grandparents, but friends warn him that it is a dangerous thing to do. Sure enough, in Mississippi two white policemen accuse father of stealing the car simply because he is black. Once he is released, he decides to continue the trip in his cousin's old Chevy. For the first time the sisters, who were raised in the North, learn what "Whites Only" signs really mean, on a trip they will never forget. On their return to Toledo, father trades in the gold Cadillac for a Mercury.

Let the Circle Be Unbroken, by Mildred Taylor. Dial, 1981.

Set in Mississippi at the height of the Great Depression, this is the story of one family's struggle to maintain their pride and independence. It is a story of physical survival and of the survival of the human spirit.

The characters, Cassie, Stacey, Little Man, and Christopher-John, experience racial antagonism and hard times, but learn from their parents the pride and self-respect they need to survive. Owning their own land means a great deal to the Logan family because it gives them freedom. But when Papa uses his land to back credit for black families to shop in Vicksburg, that freedom is threatened. Live day by day with the Logan family in the turbulent year they experience in this moving novel.

When I Crossed No-Bob, by Margaret McMullen. Houghton Mifflin, 2007.

Life as an O'Donnell is all Addy knows, and life as an O'Donnell means trouble. Tucked away in a gray patch of woods called No-Bob, the O'Donnell clan has nothing but a bad reputation. So when Addy's mama abandons her on the afternoon of Mr. Frank Russell's wedding celebration, nobody is very surprised. A reluctant Mr. Frank and his new wife take Addy in, and Addy does everything she can to prove that at least one O'Donnell has promise. But one day Addy witnesses a terrible event that brings her old world crashing into the new. As she finds herself being pulled back into No-Bob and the grips of her O'Donnell kin, Addy is faced with the biggest decision of her life. Can she somehow find the courage to do what's right, even if it means betraying one of her own?

The Drummer Boy of Vicksburg, by G. Clifton Wisler. Lodestar, 1997.

Here is a story based on the life of a real drummer boy in the Civil War. Orion Howe is thirteen when his brother enlists as a musician in a Union regiment. Both boys had been taught by their father to play the drum when they were much younger. Orion's father is already fighting for the North. Orion is expected to stay in school. Little by little the boys in his class leave to fight in the war, and Orion makes up his mind to find his brother and the 55th Illinois Infantry Regiment. The boy experiences the horrible reality of war, and he shows his true colors as a hero during the decisive battle at Vicksburg, Mississippi.

More Mississippi Titles

Armistead, John. *Return of Gabriel.* Milkweed, 2002.

Cussler, Clive. *Adventures of Vin Fiz.* Philomel, 2006.

Ernst, Kathleen. *Ghosts of Vicksburg.* White Mane, 2003.

Gray, Dianne. *Tomorrow the River.* Houghton Mifflin, 2006.

Harrell, Beatrice. *Longwalker's Journey: A Novel of the Choctaw Trail of Tears.* Dial, 1999.

Herschler, Mildred. *The Darkest Corner.* Front Street, 2000.

Jackson, Alison. *Rainmaker.* Boyds Mills, 2005.

Kenny, Kathryn. *Mystery on the Mississippi.* Random House, 1993.

Kilgore, James. *The Passage.* Peachtree, 2006.

Matas, Carol. *The War Within.* Simon & Schuster, 2001.

McMullan, Margaret. *How I Found the Strong.* Houghton Mifflin, 2004.

Rodman, Mary Ann. *Yankee Girl.* Usborne, 2005.

Rubright, Lynn. *Mama's Window.* Lee & Low, 2005.

Shalant, Phyllis. *Bartleby of the Big Bad Bayou.* Dutton, 2005.

Shalant, Phyllis. *Bartleby and the Mighty Mississippi.* Dutton, 2000.

Stark, Lynette. *Escape from Heart.* Harcourt, 2000.

Taylor, Mildred. *Roll of Thunder, Hear My Cry.* Phyllis Fogelman Books, 1977.

Vander Zee, Ruth. *Mississippi Morning.* Eerdmans, 2004.

Wiles, Deborah. *Aurora County All Stars.* Harcourt, 2007.

Missouri Fact Sheet

Capital: Jefferson City

Largest City: Kansas City

Entered the Union: August 10, 1821

Tree: Flowering dogwood

Flower: Hawthorn

Bird: Bluebird

Rivers: Missouri, Mississippi, Osage

Nickname: Show-Me State

Products: Agriculture, lead, aircraft, beer

Major Tourist Attractions:
    Gateway Arch & Museum in St. Louis
    Mark Twain Boyhood Home in Hannibal
    Lake of the Ozarks
    Silver Dollar City and Branson

Land Area: 69,704 square miles

Population 2006: 5,842,713

Motto: The Welfare of the People Shall Be the Supreme Law

Trivia

- The Gateway Arch, at 630 feet, is the tallest monument in the United States.

- The U.S. purchased Missouri from France in 1803.

- The ice cream cone was invented in St. Louis at the 1904 World's Fair.

Missouri Booktalks

Jayhawker, by Patricia Beatty. HarperCollins, 1995.

Following the lead of his hero, John Brown, Elija Tulley joins the Jayhawkers. Only thirteen, "Lije" rides with the men who cross the Missouri border from Kansas to steal slaves and take them to freedom. The opposing forces they meet are the bushwhackers, men devoted to the cause of slavery, and in one battle between the two, "Lije's" father is killed. Elija then joins a group of bushwhackers as a spy, passing news of their plans to a brave young woman. The killing and destruction of the opposing forces is made clear in the bushwhacker raid on Lawrence, Kansas, where Elija's family lives. During the terrible raid Elija comes face to face with his father's killer. Is taking revenge worth the price the boy must pay?

Hiding Mr. McNulty, by Berniece Rabe. Harcourt, 1997.

Life is hard for a sharecropper's family in the Great Depression years in southeast Missouri. Rass longs for his father's approval and affection and is befriended and encouraged by an elderly black man, Mr. McNulty, who lives nearby. When a flood destroys the family home, the landlord, Nert, orders Mr. McNulty out of his house so that Rass's family can move in. In retaliation, Mr. McNulty kills Nert's prize bull calf, hurting himself in the process, and is hidden away and cared for by Rass, who knows his father would be furious with him for putting the family in danger. Eventually Rass helps Mr. McNulty to escape and does finally gain his father's respect.

*A **Place to Belong,*** by Joan Lowery Nixon. <u>The Orphan Train Adventure Series No. 4</u>. Random House, 1996.

In 1860 the six Kelly children are sent west on the orphan train by their widowed mother, who hopes this will give them a better life. Two of the children, Danny and Peg, are adopted in St. Joseph, Missouri, by a kind and loving couple, Alfred and Olga Swenson. Olga passes away unexpectedly, and the children fear that Alfred will no longer want them with him. Danny comes up with a plan to get Alfred to send for the children's real mother in the hope that the two might marry and the children will not be sent to another home. Then a phony doctor from New York City recognizes Danny, and it looks like he may interfere with the boy's plans to be reunited with his real mother and to keep Alfred as their new father. Can Danny still carry out his plan?

Reaching Dustin, by Vicki Grove. Penguin Books, 2000.

Carly wants more than anything to become the sixth-grade newspaper editor but must write an outstanding interview story first. Unfortunately she finds that a strange and taciturn boy, Dustin Groat, is to be her subject. Dustin's gun-trading, drug-dealing family are outcasts in rural Missouri where Carly lives, and the boy is sullen and antisocial. Carly perseveres and discovers that underneath his antisocial behavior Dustin has a passion for music and a special rapport with animals, and that underneath his tough exterior is a frightened boy who needs help. Carly is ready to give it.

More Missouri Titles

Calvert, Patricia. *Betrayed.* Atheneum, 2002.

Calvert, Patricia. *Sooner.* Troll Publications, 1998.

Dahlberg, Maurine. *The Story of Jonas.* Farrar, Straus & Giroux, 2007.

Glaze, Lynn. *Seasons of the Trail.* Silver Moon, 2000.

Harness, Cheryl. *Just for You to Know.* HarperCollins, 2006.

Hermes, Patricia. *Westward to Home.* Scholastic, 2003.

Kenny, Kathryn. *Mystery on the Mississippi.* Random House, 2006.

MacBride, Roger. *Bachelor Girl.* HarperCollins, 1999.

MacBride, Roger. *Little Town in the Ozarks.* HarperCollins, 1999.

McDonald, Megan. *All the Stars in the Sky.* Scholastic, 2003.

McKissack, Pat. *A Friendship for Today.* Scholastic, 2007.

Moonshower, Candie. *Legend of Zoey.* Delacorte, 2006.

Moses, Sheila. *I, Dred Scott: A Fictional Slave Narrative Based on the Life and Legal Precedent of Dred Scott.* Margaret McElderry Books, 2005.

Nixon, Joan Lowery. *A Family Apart.* Gareth Stevens, 2000

Stone, B. J. *Ola's Wake.* Holt, Rinehart & Winston, 2000.

Tedrow, Thomas. *Children of Promise.* Nelson, 1992.

Tedrow, Thomas. *Good Neighbors.* Nelson, 1992.

Tedrow, Thomas. *Home to the Prairie.* Nelson, 1992.

Tedrow, Thomas. *Missouri Homestead.* Nelson, 1992.

Twain, Mark. *The Adventures of Huckleberry Finn.* Grosset, 2004.

Williams, Mark. *Danger Boy: Trail of Bones.* Candlewick, 2005.

Montana Fact Sheet

Capital: Helena

Largest City: Billings

Entered the Union: November 8, 1889

Tree: Ponderosa pine

Flower: Bitterroot

Bird: Western Meadowlark

Rivers: Missouri, Yellowstone, Clark Fork, Kootenai

Nickname: Treasure State

Products: Agriculture, lumber, cattle, gold, silver, oil

Major Tourist Attractions:
Little Bighorn Battlefield National Monument
Glacier National Park
The Wild West gold mining town of Virginia City

Land Area: 147,042 square miles

Population 2006: 917,621

Motto: Gold and Silver

 ## Trivia

- The name Montana comes from the Spanish word meaning mountainous.

- 57,000 Native Americans live in the state.

- There are three head of cattle for every person in Montana.

From *Reading the Fifty States: Booktalks, Response Activities, and More* by Nancy Polette. Westport, CT: Libraries Unlimited. Copyright © 2009.

Montana Booktalks

Buffalo Song, by Joseph Bruchac. Lee & Low, 2008.

Walking Coyote gently lifted the frightened buffalo calf and sang softly. Lone survivor of a herd slaughtered by white hunters, the calf was one of several buffalo orphans adopted by Walking Coyote and raised on the Flathead Indian Reservation in Montana.

For thousands of years massive herds of buffalo roamed across much of North America, but by the 1870s fewer than 1,500 of these animals remained. Hunted to the brink of extinction, the buffalo were in danger of vanishing. With reverent care, Walking Coyote and his family endeavored to bring back the buffalo herds, one magnificent creature at a time. Here is the inspiring story of the first efforts to save the buffalo, an animal sacred to Native Americans and a powerful symbol of the American West.

Wolf at the Door, by Barbara Corcoran. Simon & Schuster, 1993.

Lee McDougall does not find thirteen to be such a wonderful age, especially when she feels overshadowed by her sister, Savannah, who is both pretty and talented. Things go from bad to worse when their father decides to uproot the family in a move from Missoula to a sparsely inhabited part of Montana. Lee's mother rescues a young wolf from a roadside zoo, and Lee assumes the care of the animal. Before long she has five young wolves to care for and finds comfort as their caretaker. Meanwhile Savannah becomes the star of a local theater group, and the girls' grandmother arrives and wants to take Savannah back to Los Angeles with her. At the same time neighbors are strongly objecting to the wolves being cared for by Lee. The opposition and subsequent publicity not only unite the sisters but get the attention of someone who has the money, and agrees, to fund a wolf refuge.

Three Dog Winter, by Elizabth Van Steenwyk. Random House, 1999.

Scott McClure is twelve and a trainer of sled dogs, just as his deceased father was. To keep his father's memory alive, Scott decides to train a team of three sled dogs to continue his father's racing tradition. Unfortunately his plans change when his mother remarries and the family moves from California to Montana. Problems arise not only between Scott and his stepfather but between Scott and his stepbrother, Brad. Brad is sullen and uncooperative and has one wish, to run away and find his mother in Billings. Scott continues to train his Malamute, Kaylah, and the other dogs, little knowing the problems that will arise and that must be overcome.

The Rescue of Josh McGuire, by Ben Mikaelsen. Hyperion, 1999.

Josh and his father hunt together, but his father has changed since the death of Josh's older brother. Alcohol has now come into the mix, and on one hunting trip Josh's father shoots a female bear. The two find the bear's cub and initially Josh is warned to say nothing about it. Josh cares for the bear for a short time, until a government agency is informed of its existence and wants to take charge of it. Fearing the cub will be hurt, Josh puts it in a five gallon bucket and runs off with it on his brother's motorcycle. His dog, Mudflap, follows him as Josh struggles for survival in the days that follow.

More Montana Titles

Beechwood, Beth. *Face the Music.* Disney, 2007.

Collard, Sneed. *Dog Sense: A Novel.* Peachtree, 2005.

Ingold, Jeanette. *The Big Burn.* Harcourt, 2002.

James, Will. *Smoky the Cowhorse.* Scribner, 1926.

King, M. C. *Seeing Green.* Disney, 2007.

Lenma, Don. *When the Sergeant Came Marching Home.* Holiday House, 2008.

Maynard, Joyce. *The Cloud Chamber.* Atheneum, 2005.

McElvoy, Laurie. *Nightmare on Hannah Street.* Disney, 2007.

Philbrick, W. R. *Max the Mighty.* Blue Sky Press, 1998.

Porter, Pamela. *Sky.* Groundwood Books, 2004.

Roy, Ron. *The Ninth Nugget.* Random House, 2001.

Skurzynski, Gloria *Wolf Stalker.* National Geographic, 1997.

Thomas, Jane. *Blind Mountain.* Clarion, 2006.

Torres, Laura. *Crossing Montana.* Holt, 2002.

Yep, Laurence. *When the Circus Came to Town.* HarperCollins, 2002.

Capital: Lincoln

Largest City: Omaha

Entered the Union: March 1, 1867

Tree: Cottonwood

Flower: Goldenrod

Bird: Western meadowlark

Rivers: Missouri, Niobrara, Platte, Republican

Nicknames: Cornhusker State and Beef State

Products: Agriculture, cattle, hogs, meatpacking

Major Tourist Attractions:
Agate Fossil Beds National Monument
Girls and Boys Town
Stuhr Museum of the Prairie

Land Area: 77,354 square miles

Population 2006: 1,739,291

Motto: Equality Before the Law

 ## Trivia

- Nebraska is the only state with a single-house legislature.
- Kool-Aid™ was invented in Hastings, Nebraska.

Nebraska Booktalks

Sarah Plain and Tall, by Patricia MacLachlan. HarperCollins, 1985.

Caleb dosen't remember Mama, who died one day after he was born. But his older sister, Anna, says Papa and Mama sang "every-single-day." Now Papa doesn't sing at all. Just before spring, when the prairie will be awash with Indian paintbrush, Bride's bonnet, and violets, Papa places an ad in a newspaper for a wife. He receives an answer from a woman named Sarah, who lives in Maine. Her house is right on the coast, where she can gather moon snails, razor clams, and conch shells and watch the seals at play. She can cook flounder, oysters, and scallops fresh from the ocean waters and climb the tall spruce tree to watch ships coming in. Anna wants to know if Sarah can braid hair and make stew and, most important of all, if she sings.

Sarah writes, "I will come by train. I will wear a yellow bonnet. I am plain and tall." And so Caleb, Anna, and Papa wait.

In the spring, when prairie woodchucks and gophers are peeking out of their holes, Sarah arrives. With her is her cat, whom she calls Seal, because she is gray like the seals that swim in the sea near her home. Everyone hopes she will stay. But Sarah misses the sea, her brother, and the three old aunts who all squawk together like crows at dawn. When Sarah takes the wagon to town alone, Caleb and Anna worry. Even the turkey buzzards flying overhead seem to wonder . . . will she return? What happens tells much about happiness and hope, and what it is that makes a family.

Skylark, by Patricia MacLachlan. HarperCollins, 1994.

Skylark is the story of Papa, Sarah, Caleb, and Anna. They live on the Nebraska plain during the pioneer days. Like many during this time, they have to deal with the many hardships that pioneer life bringd. One great problem the family faces is trying to survive the drought that plagues the area. The drought forces many of the families in the surrounding area to leave Nebraska. Eventually Sarah is forced by the drought to take Anna and Caleb to Maine to live with her family. Papa has to stay behind to tend to the animals on the farm. The children, and especially Anna, find Maine to be beautiful, but Anna misses home, and as the weeks go by she begins to wonder what will happen if the rains never come. Will she and Caleb and Sarah and Papa ever be a family again?

108

My Daniel, by Pam Conrad. HarperCollins, 1989.

My name is Julia Creath Summerwaite. Being an eighty-year-old woman, I do not like to travel far from home. I am anxious, however, to see my son and his family in the East. I have not always been old, and I look forward to telling my grandchildren, Ellie and Stevie, just what my life was like as a young girl. In *My Daniel,* I have the opportunity to be with my grandchildren in the Natural History Museum, where I can tell them all about the Uncle Daniel they never knew.

As we walk from one darkened room to another in the museum, I often feel as if I have again become the Nebraska farm girl I once was. I tell Ellie and Stevie of my brother Daniel's dream of saving our family's farm by finding a dinosaur. My grandchildren are as anxious to hear my story as I am to tell it. They cannot wait to hear the details of my brother's treasure. Did he find a real dinosaur? Will he be able to keep his treasure safe and out of evil hands, or will it be too late? This is my story.

Night of the Twisters, by Ivy Ruckman. Thomas Y. Crowell, 1984.

The story begins with two boys, Dan and Arthur, at the beach. A darkening sky indicates a coming storm. Dan returns home to find his tired mother and the baby brother he resents. Dan invites Arthur to sleep over. The boys hear tornado warnings on the TV. Phone lines are down, and Dan's mother goes to check on a neighbor. The tornado hits just after the boys, with the baby, head for the basement, where water starts rising from broken pipes. Both boys are worried about their parents.

Help arrives, and they emerge to see the house entirely gone. They find Dan's mother and rescue a trapped neighbor. At the police station the family listens as National Guard helicopters cruise over the city. Dan's father arrives, and Arthur finds his parents. Dan learns that his family will be living on the farm with his grandparents until such time as the house (and the town) can be rebuilt.

More Nebraska Titles

Buchanan, Jane. *Hank's Story.* Farrar, Straus & Girouxs, 2001.

Clements, Andrew. *Room One: A Mystery or Two.* Simon & Schuster, 2006.

Cushman, Karen. *Rodzina.* Clarion, 2003.

Durbin, William. *The Journal of Sean Sullivan: A Transcontinental Railroad Worker.* Scholastic, 1999.

Gorman, Carol. *The Stumptown Kid.* Peachtree, 2005.

Gray, Diane. *Holding Up the Earth.* Houghton Mifflin, 2000.

Gray, Diane. *Together, Apart.* Houghton Mifflin, 2002.

Hart, Alison. *Anna's Blizzard.* Peachtree, 2005.

Hermes, Patricia. *Calling One Home.* Avon, 1998.

Howe, Norma. *Blue Avenger and the Theory of Everything.* Cricket Books, 2002.

Hughes, Molly. *Hoofbeats of Danger.* Pleasant Company, 1999.

LaFaye, A. *Worth.* Simon & Schuster, 2004.

Murphy, Jim. *My Face to the Wind: The Diary of Sarah Jane Price, a Prairie Teacher.* Scholastic, 2001.

Ruckman, Ivy. *In Care of Cassie Tucker.* Delacorte, 1998.

VanSteenwyk, Elizabeth. *Prairie Christmas.* Eerdmans, 2006.

Nevada Fact Sheet

Capital: Carson City

Largest City: Las Vegas

Entered the Union: October 31, 1864

Tree: Bristlecone pine

Flower: Sagebrush

Bird: Mountain bluebird

Rivers: Columbia, Humboldt, Truckee

Nicknames: Sagebrush State, Silver State, Battle Born State

Products: Gold and silver mines, tourism (gambling)

Major Tourist Attractions:
    Death Valley National Monument (extends into southwestern Nevada)
     Hoover Dam near Las Vegas
    Lake Tahoe
    Las Vegas

Land Area: 110,561 square miles

Population 2006: 2,240,150

Motto: All For Our Country

Trivia

- Cathedral Gorge got its name from its clay towers, which look like church spires.

- Camel races are held in Virginia City every September.

- Nevada has hundreds of ghost towns.

Nevada Booktalks

Weird Stories from the Lonesome Café, by Judy Cox. Harcourt, 2000.

Strange visitors come to the Lonesome Cafe in the middle of Nevada, where Sam is spending the summer. Sam's Uncle Clem has a hard time seeing what is right before his eyes. He is a writer and wants something exciting or unusual to happen so that he has something to write about. A furry stranger arrives, followed by a news crew in search of Bigfoot; a fellow named "El" arrives in a pink Cadillac; Mr. C. from up north is taking a break from his workshop duties; and a girl with her dog blows in on a tornado. Sam's uncle doesn't seem to find his visitors strange at all and hires each one of them. In the meantime, Sam's task is to distract the news crews so that they don't discover the identities of the strange visitors . . . not easy to do!

The Runaways, by Zilpha Keatley Snyder. Sagebrush, 2000.

Some parents don't do their jobs! Dani's mother means well but is passive and bumbling, and she and Dani have been stuck in Rattler Springs, Nevada, for four years. Dani decides to run away but is blackmailed by her younger neighbor, Stormy, into taking him along. This means they will have to raise enough money for the two of them to leave. The two then join up with Pixie Smithson, daughter of wealthy geologists who are too busy to have time for her. Pixie decides to run away, too, and gets the necessary funds. As the three set out to find what they think will be a better life, they eventually learn that home must be the best place to run to after all.

So B. It, by Sarah Weeks. HarperCollins, 2005.

A retarded woman who only speaks twenty-three words shows up on the doorstep of a recluse with a week-old baby. Bernadette, the recluse, takes the baby, Heidi, and her mother under her wing and cares for them. Twelve years later Heidi is consumed with wanting to know her background. She find an old camera, and the film, when developed, shows a place called Hilltop Home in New York. She sets off on a cross-country journey, sure that the answers she seeks about her mother's background will be there. Heidi does lean a great deal from her trip, but not at all what she expected to learn.

Alice, Rose and Sam, by Kathryn Lasky. Hyperion, 1999.

Alice Rose, age twelve, shares adventures with Mark Twain, who is a reporter at her father's newspaper in Virginia City, Nevada, in the 1860s. Alice is more concerned with protecting her mother's and sister's graves from coyotes than getting rich from the silver mines. In addition, she and Sam Clemens , who is not yet famous, expose the criminal activities of the Society of Seven. Other characters make this tale interesting reading as well, including Hurdy Gurdy girls, newly rich millionaires, immigrant Chinese, and crooked lawyers. Alice's wish is to earn enough money to attend a ladies' seminary in Boston. It is difficult for Sam to convince her that she is already in one of the most beautiful places on earth.

More Nevada Titles

Henry, Marguerite. *Mustang: Wild Spirit of the West.* Rand McNally, 1966.

Horowitz, Anthony. *Nightrise.* Scholastic, 2007.

Levinson, Nancy. *Snowshoe Thompson.* HarperCollins, 1992.

Philbrick, W. R. *Journal of Douglas Allen Deeds: The Donner Party Expedition.* Scholastic, 2001.

Reichart, George. *Bag of Lucky Rice.* David R. Godine, 2002.

Scordato, Ellen. *Sarah Winnemucca: Northern Paiute Writer and Diplomat.* Chelsea House, 1992.

Service, Pamela. *Vision Quest.* Atheneum, 1989.

Shahan, Sherry. *Death Mountain.* Peachtree, 2005.

Smith, Roland. *Zach's Lie.* Hyperion, 2003.

Yep, Laurence. *Dragon's Gate.* HarperCollins, 1993.

Capital: Concord

Largest City: Manchester

Entered the Union: June 21, 1788

Tree: White birch

Flower: Purple lilac

Bird: Purple finch

Rivers: Androscoggin, Merrimack, Connecticut

Nickname: Granite State

Products: Textiles, lumber, paper products

Major Tourist Attractions:
Dartmouth College Winter Carnival in Hanover
Mount Washington
White Mountain National Forest

Land Area: 9,350 square miles

Population 2006: 1,287,687

Motto: Live Free or Die

Trivia

- Has a short, 18-mile coastline along the Atlantic.

- White Mountain is the highest peak in the Northeast.

- New Hampshire was the first of the colonies to establish an independent government, six months before the Declaration of Independence.

New Hampshire Booktalks

Calico Captive, by Elizabeth George Speare. Houghton Mifflin, reissued 2001.

In the year 1754, the stillness of Charlestown, New Hampshire, is shattered by the terrifying cries of an Indian raid. On a day that promised new happiness, young Miriam Willard, her sister, and her family find themselves captives on a forest trail. They are sold by the Indians to the French, and they become servants to a French family in Montreal. Miriam and Hortense, another servant, become fast friends and share adventures on the dangerous city streets. In serving the spoiled daughter of the family, Miriam becomes acquainted with the daughter's boyfriend, Pierre, who not only helps Miriam and her sister when they are expelled from the household, but proposes marriage. Miriam is finally able to gain freedom for the family when she is befriended by the governor's wife after serving as her dressmaker. The family returns home, and Miriam and her fiancé, Phineas, are married. This is a fast-paced, exciting tale with a spunky young heroine.

First Boy, by Gary Schmidt. Henry Holt, 2005.

Grandfather, who always called Cooper his "first boy," has died, and the boy is determined to run the dairy farm he has always called home. He does his best to meet the demands of both school and the farm. Then comes the day men in dark suits are all over town. A senator and the pPresident of the United States arrive in town, and the president visits Cooper. The barn burns to the ground, and Cooper's house is broken into. To complicate matters, the president's opponent wants Cooper to travel the campaign trail with him. Does "first boy" have more than one meaning? Try this fast-paced political thriller!

The Heart of a Chief, by Joseph Bruchac. Penguin, 2001.

Eleven-year-old Chris Nicola is a Penacook Indian boy. He discovers leadership qualities he didn't know he had when he becomes embroiled in a tribal conflict over building a casino on an island that is the heart of his people and a school conflict over giving an Indian name to the school sports team. Although initially shy, Chris stands up to peer pressure at school, telling his classmates, "We didn't go away. They tried to drive us off he land but we're still here." In addition, he commits an act of protest, which causes those living on the reservation to take sides. Here is a tale of one boy who made a big difference in resolving conflicts and bringing two cultures to greater understanding of each other.

Miss Hickory, by Carolyn Sherwin Bailey. Viking, 1946.

When Great-granny Brown packed up and moved to the Women's City Club in Boston, Miss Hickory was faced with the problem of spending a severe New Hampshire winter alone. This might not have been so bad if Miss Hickory had not been a country woman, whose body was an apple-wood twig and whose head was a hickory nut. Also, she would have been better off if her house had been built of stronger material than corncobs, however neatly notched and glued together.

This is the story of how she survived those trying months, in the company of neighbors like Crow, who was tough, wise, and kindly; Bull Frog, who lost his winter clothes; Ground Hog, a surly man afraid of his own shadow; and a host of others. It is a fantasy full of the peculiar charm of the New Hampshire countryside, seen from an angle that those who are city-bound in the winter know little about.

More New Hampshire Titles

Banks, Kate. *Dillon, Dillon.* Farrar, 2002.

Blos, Joan. *A Gathering of Days: A New England Girl's Journal 1830–32 (A Novel).* Scribner, 1979.

Curry, Jane. *Moon Window.* Atheneum, 1996.

Harrar, George. *The Trouble with Jeremy Chance.* Milkweed, 2003.

Mandrell, Louise. *Peril in Evans Woods.* Summit, 1993.

Schmidt, Gary. *The Sin Eater.* Dutton, 1996.

Capital: Trenton

Largest City: Newark

Entered the Union: December 18, 1787

Tree: Red oak

Flower: Purple violet

Bird: Eastern goldfinch

Rivers: Delaware, Hudson

Nickname: Garden State

Products: Agriculture, chemicals, petroleum

Major Tourist Attractions:
　　Atlantic City beach resort
　　Edison National Historic Site in New Orange
　　Princeton University/Princeton Battlefield

Land Area: 8,721 square miles

Population 2006: 8,639,139

Motto: Liberty and Prosperity

Trivia

- The Atlantic City boardwalk is 4.5 miles long.

- Five major Revolutionary War battles were fought in New Jersey.

- The first drive-in movie theater opened in Camden in 1922.

New Jersey Booktalks

George Washington's Socks, by Elvira Woodruff. Scholastic, 1992.

Matthew was president of the Adventure Club and planning the first all-night camp out in Tony's backyard when disaster struck. Matthew can't go unless little sister Katie goes along! So that night the boys, with Katie tagging along, decide to take a walk along the river bank and find an old row boat. "This is too good a chance to pass up," Matthew thinks, as the children climb into the boat. Before long the children are lost in a velvety darkness, moved along by a strong current in a river choked with ice. And then it happens. The boat tips, and Katie goes overboard. After a frantic search, another boat appears. In the center stands George Washington, holding a wet and sleeping Katie in his arms. "Arrest the Tory spies," the general calls out, pointing to Matt's boat. The boys are speechless. Is this some TV show gag, or have they somehow gone back in time?

The Hoboken Chicken Emergency, by Daniel Pinkwater. Prentice-Hall, 1977.

Arthur Bobowicz's family likes to celebrate Thanksgiving in the traditional way, including the turkey. This year something goes wrong—the butcher loses the order for the Bobowiczs's turkey and Arthur can't find a bird for dinner in all of Hoboken. Things look bad until Arthur meets a mad professor with a live 266-pound chicken.

Arthur's mother is unwilling to cook the 266-pound chicken, which is fine with Arthur, who has grown fond of the bird. He names her Henrietta.

Henrietta's appearance unsettles the population of Hoboken, then makes them fearful, and finally causes a panic. Reason and good will save the day as the citizens cooperate to reunite Arthur and Henrietta, in this heart-warming story of a boy and a chicken facing life in the big city.

The Fighting Ground, by Avi. HarperCollins, 1984.

On April 3, 1778, America is caught up in the Revolutionary War. On this warm spring morning, not far from Trenton, New Jersey, a thirteen-year-old boy and his father are quietly tilling the sod on their farm. But the boy can think of only one thing. He wants to fight. He knows how to use a gun; why won't his father let him go? Unexpectedly the quiet is cut by the sound of a bell. An alarm is ringing at a nearby tavern. Jonathan is sent to find out what the trouble is. What he finds in the next twenty-four hours, when he does fight and is taken prisoner by three Hessian soldiers, changes his understanding of war and of life forever. The real war, he discovers, is being fought within himself.

Fire in the Sky, by Candace Ransom. Carolrhoda, 1997.

Stenny Green is nine years old, overweight, and frequently teased at school. He has two passions, the radio hero, Jack Armstrong, and the German airship the *Hindenberg*. When he hears that the *Hindenberg* will land at the Naval Air Station near his home, he tells his classmates that he will be given a tour of the airship. He skips school and makes his way to the landing site. To his horror the ship explodes and passengers are jumping from the ship to escape the flames. Stenny leads injured passengers to the safety of the hangar, finding courage he did not think he possessed. His assistance to the passengers earns him the new respect of his peers. Here is history brought to life with accurate details of a terrible disaster.

More New Jersey Titles

Avi. *Captain Grey.* Pantheon, 1977.

Bauer, A.C. *No Castles Here.* Random House, 2007.

Dixon, Franklin. *Boardwalk Bust.* Aladdin, 2005.

Green, Tim. *Football Hero.* HarperCollins, 2008.

Holm, Jennifer. *Penny from Heaven.* Thorndike Press, 2007.

Holm, Jennifer L., and Jonathan Hamel. *The Postman Always Brings Mice.* HarperCollins, 2004.

Karr, Kathleen. *Man of the Family.* Farrar, Straus & Giroux, 1999.

Lubar, David. *Dunk,* Clarion, 2002.

McDonald, Joyce. *Shades of Simon Gray.* Delacorte, 2001.

Myers, Walter Dean. *Me, Mop and the Moon Dance Kid.* Delacorte, 1988.

Papademetriou, Lisa. *The Wizard, the Witch and Two Girls from Jersey.* Razorbill, 2006.

Pinkwater, Danie. *Looking for Bobowicz: A Hoboken Chicken Story.* HarperCollins, 2004.

Porter, Connie. *Andy's Summer Place.* Pleasant Company, 2003.

Rinaldi, Ann. *A Ride into Morning: The Story of Tempe Wick.* Harcourt, 1991.

Robertson, Keith. *Henry Reed, Inc.* Viking, 1958.

Scieszka, Jon. *Oh Say, I Can't See.* Viking, 2005.

Schirripa, Steven. *Nicky Deuce: Home for the Holidays.* Delacorte, 2006.

Schumacher, Julie. *The Book of One Hundred Truths.* Delacorte, 2006.

Seuling, Barbara. *Robert Finds a Way.* Cricket Books, 2005.

Wallace, Rich. *Southpaw.* Viking, 2006.

Wallace, Rich. *Takedown.* Viking, 2006.

New Mexico Fact Sheet

Capital: Santa Fe

Largest City: Albuquerque

Entered the Union: January 6, 1912

Tree: Piñon pine

Flower: Yucca

Bird: Roadrunner

Rivers: Gila, Pecos, Rio Grande

Nickname: Empire State

Products: Oil, natural gas, copper, silver uranium

Major Tourist Attractions:
Carlsbad Caverns National Park
Bandelier National Monument
Los Alamos Bradbury Science Hall and Museum
Santa Fe Art Colony

Land Area: 121,589 square miles

Population 2006: 1,874,614

Motto: It Grows as It Goes

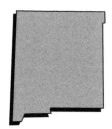

Trivia

- Mud-baked adobe pueblos found in Taos can last hundreds of years.

- Santa Fe was founded by the Spanish 11 years before the Pilgrims landed at Plymouth Rock.

New Mexico Booktalks

Sing Down the Moon, by Scott O'Dell. Houghton Mifflin, 1970.

The spring that came to the Canyon de Chelly in 1864 was abundant, for the fields and orchards of the Navajos who lived there promised a rich harvest. The sheep were lambing and the sky was bright blue. But all was shattered when the white soldiers burned the crops, destroyed the fruit trees, and forced the Navajos out of the canyon to join their Indian brothers on the devastating long march to Fort Sumner.

Through the eyes of Bright Morning, a young Navajo girl, we see what can happen to human beings when they are uprooted from the life they know. She tells the story of the proud and able Tall Boy, the youth she expected to marry, who is maimed not only by a physical wound, but by a spiritual wound as well. And she tells of the other men of the tribe who, on the march along the "Trail of Tears," lose their will along with their way of life. It is a story with tragic overtones, a story of the breaking of the human spirit. And yet fortunately, then as now, there were a few possessed of inner strength based on hope; Bright Morning was one of them.

Meet Josephina, an American Girl, by Valerie Tripp. Pleasant Company, 2000.

This is one of a series of books about nine-year-old Josephina Montoya, who lives with her father and sisters on a ranch near Santa Fe, New Mexico, in 1824. Her mother has died and her aunt, Tia Delores, arrives to become a member of the family. Josephina is enchanted with the piano her aunt brings with her. Joephina and her sisters struggle to help their father run the ranch while at the same time helping Tia Delores become a member of the family. The family must cope with hardships, including a flash flood, but they work together to overcome difficulties, including Josephina's fear of a goat.

Kokopelli's Flute, by Will Hobbs. Simon & Schuster, 2005.

Tep Jones has always felt the magic of Picture House, an Anasazi cliff dwelling near the seed farm where he lives with his parents. But he could never have imagined what would happen to him on the night of a lunar eclipse, when he finds a bone flute left behind by grave robbers. Tep falls under the spell of a powerful ancient magic that traps him at night in the body of an animal. Only by unraveling the mysteries of Picture House can Tep save himself and his desperately ill mother. Does the enigmatic old Indian who calls himself Cricket hold the key to unlocking the secrets of the past? And can Tep find the answers in time?

Dance of the Crystal Skull, by Norma Lehr. Lerner Books, 1999.

How might you feel if forces pulled you from the modern to the ancient world? Does each world have something to offer? While visiting her aunt' s friend, Concha, in New Mexico, eleven-year-old Kathy Wickham comes across a mysterious jawless skull, an ancient Indian artifact. The skull disappears from Concha's home, and a local healing woman, Luna, is the prime suspect. Luna is strongly against modern medicine in any form, practicing the ancient ways of healing. In the search for the skull Kathy discovers the Cave of Knowing and is told that she is the one chosen to solve an old conflict. She finds herself pulled between two worlds and searching for ways to bring past and present ways together.

More New Mexico Titles

Anaya, Rudolfo. *My Land Sings: Stories from the Rio Grande.* Morrow, 1999.

Broach, Elsie. *Desert Crossing.* Henry Holt, 2006.

Dewey, Jennifer. *Wildlife Rescue.* Boyds Mills, 1994.

Fleischman, Sid. *Disappearing Act.* Greenwillow, 2003.

Hulme, Joy. *Climbing the Rainbow.* HarperCollins, 2004.

Hulme, Joy. *Through the Open Door.* HarperCollins, 2000.

Hunt, Laura. *The Abernathy Boys.* HarperCollins, 2004.

Klages. Ellen. *The Green Glass Sea.* Viking, 2006.

Kudlinski, Kathleen. *Spirit Catchers.* Watson-Guptill, 2004.

Mazzio, Joann. *Leaving Eldorado.* Houghton Mifflin, 1993.

O'Dell, Scott. *The Captive.* Houghton Mifflin, 1979.

Ryan, Pam M. *Becoming Naomi Leon.* Scholastic, 2004.

Talbert, Marc. *Small Change.* DK, Inc., 2000.

Taschek, Karen. *House of Seven Moons.* University of New Mexico Press, 2005.

Thurlo, Aimee. *The Spirit Line.* Viking, 2004.

Tripp, Valerie. *Changes for Josephina.* Pleasant Company, 2004.

Tripp, Valerie. *Josephina Learns a Lesson.* Pleasant Company, 2000.

Tripp, Valerie. *Just Josephina.* Pleasant Company, 2002.

Tripp, Valerie. *Reward for Josephina.* Pleasant Company, 2000.

Capital: Albany

Largest City: New York

Entered the Union: July 26, 1788

Tree: Sugar Maple

Flower: Rose

Bird: Bluebird

Rivers: Genesee, Hudson, Mohawk

Nickname: Empire State

Products: Dairy, banking, finance, trade

Major Tourist Attractions:
Adirondack Park
Corning Glass Center
Niagara Falls
New York City

Land Area: 54,556 square miles

Population 2006: 19,306,183

Motto: It Grows as It Goes

Trivia

- New York City was the capital of the U.S., 1785–1790.

- The Statue of Liberty was a gift from the people of France.

- The Empire State Building has 103 floors.

From *Reading the Fifty States: Booktalks, Response Activities, and More*
by Nancy Polette. Westport, CT: Libraries Unlimited. Copyright © 2009.

New York Booktalks

My Side of the Mountain, by Jean Craighead George. HarperCollins, 1972.

Sam Gribley knew that somewhere up in the Catskill Mountains there was an old beech tree with the name Gribley carved into it. His great-grandfather had tried to farm the land around it but had given up. It still belonged to the Gribleys, though, and Sam was emphatic about going there and living off the land. He left the city with $40.00, a penknife, a ball of cord, an axe, and some flint and tinder for starting a fire. He hitched rides from New York to the Catskills.

The first night Sam sat in the piney air and whittled a hook to catch some fish. Even though he caught the fish, he couldn't start a fire. He remembered what the man had told him about using the flint and steel—"A hard brisk strike is best"—but the sparks flew everywhere. He settled down to sleep, but a whip-poor-will started to call and he got very little sleep that night, the first night of Sam's unforgettable mountain adventure.

Monkey Island, by Paula Fox. Orchard, 1991.

"Monkey Island! Monkey Island!" the goons howled. In the wintry light, Clay could see that they held chains and baseball bats. He knew he should run.

"We got to get out of here," Buddy said urgently. And Calvin muttered, "The stump people . . . out for a night's sport."

Over the weeks that Clay Garrity had slept in the park with others of New York's "homeless," Buddy and Calvin had become his family. Somewhere in the vast city, Clay's real father wandered, jobless and unable to bear it; his mother, too, was gone now from the welfare hotel that had been their shelter. Desperation had overcome her and swept her away. Clay couldn't leave the streets, for if he did he might never find Ma or Daddy again.

"Monkey Island! Where the monkeys live!"

He and Calvin and Buddy must run to save themselves, run from the haven of the park, run among the shadows that were other people "trying to find better ways of sleeping on stone" at the entrances of buildings. Clay had learned to see them. At age eleven, he might become a shadow himself. But if he did not run, he might not live at all.

The Cricket in Times Square, by George Selden. Farrar, Straus & Giroux, 1960.

Chester Cricket arrives in New York City's Times Square Subway Station one June in a picnic basket. He had climbed in while the owners were picnicking in Chester's native Connecticut. Mario Bellini, whose parents operate an unprofitable newsstand in the station, finds him and puts him in the newsstand as a pet. Tucker Mouse and Harry Cat, who share a home in a nearby drainpipe, become his good friends. Chester has a satisfying summer with these two friends and with Mario, who plays games with him and buys him a cricket cage in Chinatown.

In August, Chester begins to chirp. One night while he, Tucker, and Harry are having a dinner party complete with background music from the Bellinis' small radio, the three friends make a startling discovery: Chester has the ability to imitate perfectly any music he hears once on the radio. The next day the Bellinis overhear him playing an Italian folksong he had heard the previous evening, leading to a series of amazing events.

The Garden of Eve, by K. L. Going. Harcourt, 2007.

Evie reluctantly moves with her widowed father to Beaumont, New York, where he has bought an apple orchard, dismissing rumors that the town is cursed and the trees haven't borne fruit in decades. Evie doesn't believe in things like curses and fairy tales anymore. But odd things happen in Beaumont. Evie meets a boy who claims to be dead and receives a mysterious seed as an eleventh birthday gift. Once planted, the seed grows into a tree overnight, but only Evie and the dead boy can see it, or go where it leads. A tale with spine-tingling chills.

More New York Titles

Auch, Mary Jane. *One Handed Catch.* Henry Holt, 2006.

Avi. *The Seer of Shadows.* HarperCollins, 2008.

Baker, Sharon. *A Nickel, a Trolley, a Treasure House.* Viking, 2007.

Bruchac, Joseph. *Return of Skeleton Man.* HarperCollins, 2006.

Collins, Suzanne. *Gregor and the Marks of Secret.* Scholastic, 2006.

DeFelice, Cynthia. *Ghost of Poplar Point.* Farrar, Straus & Giroux, 2007.

Edwards, Julie. *The Great American Mousical.* HarperCollins, 2006.

Friedman, D. Dina. *Playing Dad's Song.* Farrar, Straus & Giroux, 2006.

Giff, Patricia. *Eleven.* Wendy Lamb Books, 2008.

Irving, Washington. *The Legend of Sleepy Hollow.* Atheneum, reissued 2007.

Kimmel, Elizabeth. *The Top Job.* Dutton, 2007.

Knight, Joan. *Charlotte in New York.* Chronicle Books, 2006.

McCall, John. *The Blackout Gang.* Razorbill, 2006.

McKissack, Patricia. *A Song for Harlem.* Viking, 2007.

Moses, Sheila. *Return of Buddy Bush.* Atheneum, 2006.

Nimmo, Jenny. *Emlyn's Moon.* Orchard Books, 1987.

Osborne, Mary Pope. *Night of the New Magicians.* Scholastic, 2006.

Schwabach Karen. *A Pickpocket's Tale.* Random House, 2006.

Schwartz, Ellen. *Stealing Home.* Tundra, 2006.

Tate, Eleanor. *Celeste's Harlem Renaissance.* Little, Brown, 2007.

Weston, Carol. *Melanie in Manhattan.* Knopf, 2005.

North Carolina Fact Sheet

Capital: Raleigh

Largest City: Charlotte

Entered the Union: November 2, 1889

Tree: Pine

Flower: Dogwood

Bird: Cardinal

Rivers: Neuse, Yadkin, Roanoke

Nickname: Tar Heel State

Products: Textiles, furniture

Major Tourist Attractions:
    Biltmore House and Gardens
    Blue Ridge Parkway
    Great Smoky Mountains National Park
    Ocracoke Island

Land Area: 48,718 square miles

Population 2006: 8,856,505

Motto: To Be Rather Than to Seem

 ## Trivia

- North Carolina was the last state to join the Confederacy.

- An American flag 65 feet tall and 114 feet wide flies in the town of Gastonia and can be seen for 30 miles.

From *Reading the Fifty States: Booktalks, Response Activities, and More*
by Nancy Polette. Westport, CT: Libraries Unlimited. Copyright © 2009.

North Carolina Booktalks

Greetings from Nowhere, by Barbara O'Connor. Farrar, Straus & Giroux, 2008.

Aggie isn't expecting visitors at the Sleepy Time Motel in the Great Smoky Mountains. Since Harold died, she is all alone with her cat, Ugly, and keeping up with the bills and repairs has become next to impossible, The pool is empty, the garden is overgrown, and not a soul has come to stay in nearly three months. When she reluctantly places a "For Sale" ad in the newspaper, Aggie doesn't know that Kirby and his mom will need a room when their car breaks down on the way to Kirby's new reform school. Or that Loretta and her parents will arrive in her dad's plumbing company van on a trip meant to honor the memory of Loretta's birth mother. Or that Clyde Dover will answer the ad in such a hurry and move in with his daughter, Willow, looking for a brand new life to replace the one that was fractured when Willow's mom left. Perhaps the biggest surprise of all is that Aggie and her guests find just the friends they need in the shabby motel in the middle of nowhere.

The Baptism, by Sheila P. Moses. Margaret McElderry Books, 2007.

When you turn twelve in Occoneechee Neck in Jackson, North Carolina, everything changes. You get to do stuff you couldn't do when you were eleven. And it means it's time to be baptized.

Twin brothers Leon and Luke ?Curry turned twelve last month. Mama has given them one week in which to do right to cleanse themselves of their sinning ways and get themselves ready for the baptism. But that is only if they can keep out of trouble for a whole week. That is easier said than done when you have lost your daddy and have an unwanted stepfather; when you have a bullying big brother; and when it's summertime and all you want to do is go fishing. The twins do stick together to face the odds and save themselves while unexpectedly saving their family in a week's time.

Who Comes with Cannons? by Patricia Beatty. William Morrow, 1992.

When Truth Hopkins's father dies, she goes to live with her uncle and his family on their North Carolina farm. Like Truth, the Bardwells are Quakers. They oppose slavery but refuse to take up arms in the Civil War that is now being waged to end this inhuman institution. Then one day a runaway slave takes refuge on the Bardwell farm and, to Truth's amazement, her uncle hides him from the slave catchers. Even more puzzling, he asks her to accompany him when he delivers a wagonload of hay to a neighbor later that night. This ride, and the wagon's real cargo, bound eventually for Canada, involve Truth in a mysterious and dangerous underground movement that would eventually help almost 100,000 slaves to freedom, and shows how Truth can help further the cause of freedom without using a rifle.

Letters from a Slave Girl: The Story of Harriet Jacobs, by Mary E. Lyons. Charles Scribner's Sons, 1992.

"Freedom! The word tastes like Christmas when I say it out loud. Like a juicy orange or a sweetened cup of milk."

Harriet Jacobs has lived her entire life in slavery. Daughter and granddaughter of slaves in North Carolina, she has known no other existence. Now in 1825 with the death of her mistress, the motherly Margaret Horniblow, who has taught young Harriet to read, there is hope that Miss Horniblow's will has provided for Harriet's freedom. Crushed to find out the will has merely transferred control of Harriet to Margaret Horniblow's sister and her menacing husband, Harriet sees escape to freedom in the North as her only goal. But numerous ordeals face her before she experiences that glorious moment. Through Harriet's riveting letters the reader shares her fears, struggles, and dreams. *Letters from a Slave Girl* reveals in poignant detail what thousands of African American women endured in the United States little more than a century ago.

More North Carolina Titles

Alphin, Elaine. *Ghost Soldier.* Henry Holt, 2001.

Coleman, Evelyn. *Mystery of the Dark Tower.* Pleasant Company, 2000.

Coleman, Evelyn. *Shadows on Society Hill.* Pleasant Company, 2007.

Conly, Jane. *What Happened on Planet Kid?* Henry Holt, 2000.

Davis, C. L. *Christmas Barn.* Pleasant Company, 2001.

Doyle, Bill. *Nabbed! 1925: Journal of G. Todd Fitzmorgan.* Little, Brown, 2006.

Ernst, Kathleen. *Betrayal at Cross Creek.* Pleasant Company, 2004.

Gantos, Jack. *Jack Adrift.* Farrar, Straus & Giroux, 2003.

Hicks, Betty. *Get Real.* Roaring Brook Press, 2006.

Holmes, Elizabeth. *Pretty Is.* Dutton, 2007.

Karr, Kathleen. *World's Apart.* Marshall Cavendish, 2005.

Madden, Kerry. *Gentle's Holler.* Viking, 2005.

O'Connor, Barbara. *How to Steal a Dog: A Novel.* Farrar, Straus & Giroux, 2007.

Oughton, Jerrie. *Perfect Family.* Houghton Mifflin, 2000.

Platt, Richard. *Pirate Diary: The Journal of Jake Carpenter.* Candlewick, 2001.

Porter, Connie. *Addie Learns a Lesson.* Pleasant Company, 2000.

White, Ruth. *Buttermilk Hill.* Farrar, Straus & Giroux, 2006.

North Dakota Fact Sheet

Capital: Bismarck

Largest City: Fargo

Entered the Union: November 2, 1889

Tree: American elm

Flower: Wild prairie rose

Bird: Western meadowlark

Rivers: James, Missouri, Red

Nicknames: Sioux State, Flickertail State, Peace Garden State

Products: Wheat, barley, oats

Major Tourist Attractions:
The Badlands, with carved rocks in unusual shapes
Fort Abraham Lincoln State Park
The International Peace Garden

Land Area: 70,700 square miles

Population 2006: 635,867

Motto: Liberty and Union, Now and Forever, One and Inseparable

Trivia

- In some years North Dakota leads all states in wheat production.

- Farms cover more than 90 percent of North Dakota's land.

- A National Buffalo Museum is located in Jamestown, North Dakota.

North Dakota Booktalks

Jake's Orphan, by Margaret Brooke. Simon & Schuster, 2001.

In 1926 Tree, an orphan, had mixed feelings about being adopted. He wanted to belong to a family, but when Mr. Gunderson, a farmer, agrees to take Tree, he refuses to take Acorn, Tree's younger brother. Mr. Gunderson is a strict taskmaster and finds fault with almost everything Tree does. The one redeeming factor on the Gunderson farm is Jake, Mr. Gunderson's brother. Jack and Tree become fast friends. Acorn runs away from the orphanage and shows up on the farm, and Jake knows he will be in even greater trouble when Mr. Gunderson sees Acorn. Jake, however, proves that a friend in need can be a friend indeed.

Jakarta Missing, by Jane Kurtz. Greenwillow, 2001.

Dakar is the child of American parents who lived in Africa. She has never lived outside of Africa and has a huge adjustment to make when her parents move the family to Cottonwood, North Dakota. Fitting in a new school, making new friends, and facing problems alone when her parents are gone for long periods of time all pale when she learns that her older sister Jakarta, who was left behind at a boarding school in Kenya, is missing.

Dakar is a worrywart. Where could Jakarta be? What terrible things have happened to her? Are Dakar's parents in danger? Why are they gone for such long periods of time? When Jakarta eventually joins the family, Dakar still worries about fitting in a new life, until she accepts her father's philosophy that life can be an adventure, wherever you are.

Grasshopper Summer, by Ann Turner. Macmillan, 1989.

Safe. We were safe. We got the land from the government and it was ours as long as we planted ten acres, built a house, and stayed for five years. That didn't sound so hard. No Northerners could come and take it away. We wouldn't look out one day and see our bottomland all shrunk to nothing, the way Grandpa did after the war.

Sam White likes Kentucky. He likes fishing and joking with his friends; he likes the cool shade under the trees in summer; he likes his grandmother's peach pies and his grandfather's soldierly ways. But Sam's father is restless, still haunted by the bloodshed of the Civil War, and resolves to make a new life for himself and his family in the Dakota Territory. Sam can't stand the idea of leaving behind his grandparents and the orderly, familiar life of their farm.

The journey west is long and hard, and when the White family finally reach the Dakotas, things are harder still. To Sam the sod house they are building feels like a grave, and the endless prairie sky seems empty and unwelcoming. But he does his best to stop missing Kentucky and begins to look forward to their first harvest. Then the grasshoppers come, eating every green thing in sight . . . .

How Sam and his family meet the challenge of this harsh land is an engrossing story of love and courage in the face of tremendous odds.

By the Shores of Silver Lake, by Laura Ingalls Wilder. HarperCollins, 1939.

Laura Ingalls and her family move from the little house on the prairie to the wilderness of the unsettled Dakota territory. Here Pa works on the new railroad until he finds a homestead claim that is perfect for their new house. Laura takes her first train ride as she, her sisters, and her mother come out to live with Pa on the shores of Silver Lake. After a lonely winter in the surveyor's house, Pa puts up the first building in what will soon be a brand new town. The family's covered wagon travels are finally over.

More North Dakota Titles

Brooks, Bruce. *Moves Make the Man.* HarperCollins, 1996.

Calvert, Patricia. *Betrayed.* Atheneum, 2002.

Fitzgibon, Sally. *Lizzie's Storm.* Fitzhenry & Whiteside, 2004.

Lawlar, Laurie. *Wind on the River.* Jamestown, 2000.

Matthaei, Gay. *Sketchbook of Thomas Blue Eagle.* Chronicle, 2001.

Naylor, Patricia Reynolds. *Blizzard's Wake.* Atheneum, 2002.

Osborne, Mary Pope. *Buffalo Before Breakfast.* Random House, 1999.

Rinaldi, Ann. *My Heart Is in the Ground: Diary of Nanny Little Rose, a Sioux Girl.* Scholastic, 1999.

Rylant, Cynthia. *A Fine White Dust.* Bradbury, 1986.

Schultz, Jan. *Battle Cry.* Carolrhoda, 2006.

Sneve, Virginia Driving Hawk. *Bad River Boys: A Meeting of the Lakota Sioux with Lewis & Clark.* Holiday House, 2005.

Spooner, Michael. *Last Child.* Henry Holt, 2005.

Taylor, Don. *Old Sam, Dakota Trotter.* Ignatius Press, 2001.

Weitzman, David. *Thrashin' Time: Harvest Days in the Dakotas.* David R. Godine, 1991.

Whelan, Gloria. *Miranda's Last Stand.* HarperCollins, 2000.

Ohio Fact Sheet

Capital: Columbus

Largest City: Columbus

Entered the Union: March 1, 1803

Tree: Buckeye

Flower: Scarlet carnation

Bird: Cardinal

Rivers: Cuyahoga, Miami, Sandusky, Ohio

Nickname: Buckeye State

Products: Steel, automobiles, aircraft, chemicals, plastics

Major Tourist Attractions:
  Mound City Group National Monument (Indian Burial Grounds)
  Neil Armstrong Air and Space Museum (Wapakoneta)
  Pro Football Hall of Fame (Canton)

Land Area: 44,825 square miles

Population 2006: 11,435,800

Motto: With God, All Things Are Possible

Trivia

- Seven U.S. presidents were born in Ohio.

- The Cincinnati Reds was the world's first professional baseball team.

- Lifesaver candy was invented in Cleveland in 1912.

Ohio Booktalks

The House of Dies Drear, by Virginia Hamilton. Macmillan, 1968.

The Small family leases an old Ohio house that is reportedly haunted by the runaway slaves who died there during the days of the Underground Railroad. Thomas Small, the son, is afraid of and resents old Pluto, the caretaker. Strange shapes appear at night, and warning signs are left on doors. The family is not welcomed in the community, and Thomas becomes more and more unhappy. Then a series of events leads to the discovery of a treasure trove deep in a cave underground, guarded for many years by Pluto. The Darrow boys want to run Pluto out and get the treasure for themselves. Pluto's son, with the help of the Smalls, foils their plan, and the House of Dies Drear finally gives up its secrets.

Me and the Pumpkin Queen, by Marlane Kennedy. Greenwillow, 2007.

Mildred is a very focused eleven-year-old, very focused on giant pumpkins. She is growing the pumpkins for her mother, who fell ill before she had the chance to enter in the Circleville, Ohio, Pumpkin Show weigh-off. After four disastrous growing seasons, Mildred is hoping finally to have a flawless pumpkin to enter in the contest . . . as long as busybody Aunt Arlene doesn't interfere too much and Daddy doesn't need too much help at his veterinary office, and her best friend Jacob can pitch in with some last minute help, and the dogs don't trample the seedlings, and the weather cooperates. If nothing else goes wrong, Mildred is sure to have a winner . . . or is she?

M.C. Higgins the Great, by Virginia Hamilton. Macmillan, 1999.

For countless generations the Higgins family has lived on Sarah Mountain. The mountain is named for M.C.s great-grandmother, who escaped to the mountain as a runaway slave. When M.C. looks out from atop the gleaming forty-foot pole that his father planted in the mountain for him as a gift for swimming the Ohio River, he sees only the rolling hills and shady valleys that stretch out for miles in front of him. And M.C. knows why his father never wants the family to leave. But when M.C. looks behind he sees only the massive remains of strip mining, a gigantic heap of dirt and debris perched threateningly on a cliff above his home. And M.C. knows they cannot stay. So when two strangers arrive in the hills, one bringing the promise of fame in the world beyond the mountains and the other the revelation that choice and action lie within his grasp, M.C.'s life is changed forever.

Freedom River, by Doreen Rappaport. Hyperion, 2000.

Many years earlier John Parker, a runaway slave, crossed the Ohio river to find freedom in the small town of Ripley. As the years passed, John Parker became a successful businessman, but he never forgot the plight of those bound by the chains of slavery. Time and again John Parker risked his life to lead runaway slaves across a thin stretch of river to safety in Ohio. Each trip required courage, planning, and faith. Freedom River describes one suspense-filled incident in the life of John Parker that brings alive the work of the Underground Railroad.

More Ohio Titles

Carbone, Elisa. *Night Running.* Knopf, 2008.

Cheng, Andrea. *Eclipse.* Front Street Books, 2006.

Cheng, Andrea. *Honeysuckle House.* Front Street Books, 2004.

DeFelice, Cynthia. *Bringing Ezra Back.* Farrar, Straus & Giroux, 2006.

Durant, Lynda. *Turtle Clan Journey.* Clarion, 1999.

Ernst, Kathleen. *Danger at the Zoo.* American Girl, 2005.

Fitzgerald, Dawn. *Getting in the Game.* Roaring Brook Press, 2005.

Giblin, James. *The Boy Who Saved Cleveland.* Holt, 2006.

Green, Stephanie. *Queen Sophie Hartley.* Clarion, 2005.

Greenberg, Dan. *Secrets of Dripping Fang.* Harcourt, 2006.

Hamilton, Virginia. *Time Pieces.* Blue Sky Press, 2002.

Mackall, Dandi. *Rudy Rides the Rails.* Sleeping Bear Press, 2001.

Naylor, Phyllis Reynolds. *Who Won the War?* Delacorte, 2006.

Pearsall, Shelley. *Crooked River.* Knopf, 2005.

Reeder, Carolyn. *Captain Kate.* Avon, 2005.

Roos, Stephen. *Recycling George.* Simon & Schuster, 2002.

Tripp, Valerie. *Changes for Kit: A Winter Story.* Pleasant Company, 2001.

Tripp, Valerie. *Kit's Home Run.* Pleasant Company, 2002.

VanLeeuwen, Jean. *Cabin on Trouble Creek.* Dial, 2004.

Woodsen, Jacqueline. *Lena.* Delacorte, 1999.

Zinnen, Linda. *The Dragons of Spratt, Ohio.* HarperCollins, 2004.

Oklahoma Fact Sheet

Capital: Oklahoma City

Largest City: Oklahoma City

Entered the Union: ~~March 1, 1803~~ November 16, 1907

Tree: Redbud

Flower: Oklahoma rose

Bird: Scissor-tailed flycatcher

Rivers: Arkansas, Canadian, Red

Nickname: Sooner State

Products: Wheat, cattle, oil, natural gas

Major Tourist Attractions:
National Cowboy Hall of Fame in Oklahoma City
Chickasaw National Recreation Area
Sequoyah State Park on Fort Gibson Lake

Land Area: 69,898 square miles

Population 2006: 3,579,212

Motto: Labor Conquers All Things

Trivia

- Ten percent of the population are Native Americans.

- Oklahoma City boasted the world's first parking meter, in 1935.

- An annual seed spitting contest is held in Pauls Valley.

Summer of the Monkeys, by Wilson Rawls. Doubleday, 1976.

Jay Berry is fourteen years old and lives with his family in the Ozark Mountains, part of the Cherokee Nation land in the 1800s. The family is poor . . . too poor to afford the operation needed to mend his sister's twisted leg.

Jay dreams of owning two things, a .22 rifle and a pony. But there is no money for such dreams . . . until, that is, a band of monkeys escapes from a wrecked circus train and takes up residence in the hills. A reward is offered for their capture, a huge sum of over $100. If Jay can catch the monkeys, his dreams will come true.

Jay finds the monkeys but soon discovers that capturing them will be no easy task. The leader of the monkey band, Jimbo, seems almost human in outsmarting Jay at every turn. Success and Jay's dream come in a way no one would ever have imagined. The lessons of life that Jay learns during the *Summer of the Monkeys* are those for all young readers to ponder.

Out of the Dust, by Karen Hesse. Scholastic, 1997.

The Great Depression is in full swing, and no one knows that better than fourteen-year-old Billie Jo. She longs to leave her father's failing farm and dreams of becoming a famous concert pianist. But dust is everywhere, in the eyes and between the teeth and in every crook and cranny of every building, including the hot, dusty schoolhouse. A fire causes the death of Billie's mother, and the girl's dreams for the future are shattered: in attempting to save her mother, Billie Jo burns her hands so badly that they are nothing but swollen lumps. Yet a ray of hope remains as this plucky heroine copes with the blows life has dealt her.

Where the Red Fern Grows, by Wilson Rawls. Doubleday, 1961.

Billy lives in the Ozark Mountains in a log cabin. The land runs from the foothills of the mountains to the banks of a rolling river, where Billy spends most of his time, hunting and tracking anything he can find; frogs, minnows, crawfish, snakes, lizards, rats, and anything else that isn't quick enough or smart enough to get away. As he gets older his taste in hunting grows also. He wants to hunt ringtails but needs a good pair of coonhounds. For a whole year he begs his parents to buy a pair of dogs, but they just can't afford to.

Finally Billy decides to somehow earn the money himself. He starts by selling small game furs that he has trapped in the canebrakes behind the fields. He sells minnows, crawfish, berries, and vegetables, too. It takes two whole years of hard work, but Billy finally saves the $50.00 needed to buy a pair of redbone coonhound pups. He trains them to hunt Mister Ringtail, and everyone knows that my Little Ann and Old Dan are the best around.

The boy and his dogs have all types of adventures, some good and some bad. One of those times is when the Pritchard brothers bet that his dogs can't tree the "ghost coon." The "ghost coon" got his name because no dog had ever treed him before. The rumor was that he just disappeared into thin air whenever a dog got him up a tree. Billy has faith in his dogs, though, so he takes the bet. Something unexpected happens that night, something Billy will never forget, and he wishes he had never made that bet.

Ethan Between Us, by Anna Myers. Sagebrush, 2000.

A friendship comes apart when handsome Ethan, an accomplished pianist, arrives in Collins Creek, Oklahoma. He claims he was taught by a long dead composer. The doctors label Ethan schizophrenic. Clare deserts her best friend, Liz, to help Ethan find the truth. In turn, a betrayed Liz sets off a chain of tragic events that are felt throughout the town before the girls' friendship is restored.

A thoughtful novel for older readers.

More Oklahoma Titles

Bailey, Len. *Clabbernapper.* Starscape, 2005.

Beard, Darlene. *The Babs Switch Story.* Farrar, Straus & Giroux, 2002.

Beard, Darlene. *The Flim Flam Man.* Farrar, Straus & Giroux, 1998.

Bruchac, Joseph. *Geronimo.* Scholastic, 2006.

Connell, Kate. *Adventures of Patty and Earl Buckler.* National Geographic, 2004.

Connell, Kate. *Hoping for Rain.* National Geographic, 2004.

Durbin, William. *The Journal of C.J. Jackson: A Dust Bowl Migrant.* Scholastic, 2002.

Gilbert, Barbara. *Paper Trail.* Front Street Books, 2000.

Griffis, Molly. *The Feester Filibuster.* Eakins, 2000.

Griffis, Molly. *The Rachel Resistance.* Eakins, 2001.

Griffis, Molly. *Simon Says.* Eakins, 2004.

Harrell, Beatrice. *Longwalker's Journey: A Novel of the Choctaw Trail of Tears.* Dial, 1999.

Hunt, Laura. *The Abernathy Boys.* HarperCollins, 2004.

McCaughrean, Geraldine. *Stop the Train! A Novel.* HarperCollins, 2001.

Myers, Anna. *Spotting the Leopard.* Walker, 1996.

Myers, Anna. *Tulsa Burning.* Walker, 2002.

Myers, Walter Dean. *The Journal of Joshua Loper, a Black Cowboy.* Scholastic, 1999.

Porter, Tracey. *Treasures in the Dust.* HarperCollins, 1997.

Wallace, Bill. *Coyote Autumn.* Holiday House, 2000.

Wallace, Bill. *The Dog Who Thought He Was Santa.* Holiday House, 2007.

Oregon Fact Sheet

Capital: Salem

Largest City: Portland

Entered the Union: February 14, 1859

Tree: Douglas Fir

Flower: Oregon grape

Bird: Western meadowlark

Rivers: Deschutes, Willamette, Columbia

Nickname: Beaver State

Products: Lumber, wood, and paper products

Major Tourist Attractions:
   Crater Lake
   For Clatsop National Memorial
   John Day Fossil Beds National Monument
   Oregon Dunes

Land Area: 44,820 square miles

Population 2006: 12,440,620

Motto: She Flies With Her Own Wings

 ## Trivia

- Oregon contains more standing lumber than any other state.

- Lewis and Clark reached the mouth of the Columbia River in 1805.

- Many Bigfoot sightings have occurred in the woods of Oregon.

From *Reading the Fifty States: Booktalks, Response Activities, and More* by Nancy Polette. Westport, CT: Libraries Unlimited. Copyright © 2009.

Oregon Booktalks

The Hearts of Horses, by Molly Gloss. Houghton Mifflin, 2007.

In the winter of 1917, when a young woman shows up on his doorstep looking for work breaking horses, George Bliss hires her on. Many of his regular hands are off fighting the war, and he glimpses beneath her showy rodeo garb a shy but feisty girl with a serious knowledge of horses.

So begins the irresistible tale of nineteen-year-old Martha Lesson, a female horse whisperer trying to make it in a man's world. At the time it was thought that the only way to break a horse was to "buck the wild out of him," but when the ranchers in this remote county of eastern Oregon witness Martha talking in sweet tones to horses believed beyond breaking and getting miraculous results, she earns the respect of the community. For older readers.

The Barn, by Avi. Orchard Books, 1994.

The year is 1885 and Ben, who is nine and the youngest in the family, is away at boarding school He is a very bright boy, but his studies are interrupted when his father is laid low with a stroke and Ben is called home. Despite his age, Ben becomes a leader and seeks ways to communicate with his father while handing out various chores to other family members. Before long Ben becomes obsessed with building a barn planned earlier by his father. He thinks that if they complete the almost too difficult task, his father's health will improve. Ben is intelligent enough to know in his heart that there is no connection between completion of the barn and his father's health, but his passion and obsession drive him to complete the task.

Nekomah Creek, by Linda Crew. Delacorte, 1991.

Suppose your family isn't "normal" like other families. Your mother goes to work and your father keeps house and looks after the lively twins. Neatness is not important in the Hummer household. Robert is nine, and his teacher is so concerned that he would rather read than take part in sports that she sends him to the school counselor. Robert knows that it was the counselor, Mrs. Van Gent, who had his friend, Amber, placed in a foster home. He fears that if the counselor discovers his own unconventional home, he and his siblings might be placed in foster care. Then a terrible thing happens. Robert's father offers to fix a very special meal in the Hummer home for the highest bidder at an auction. The highest bidder turns out to be Mrs. Van Gent. Now Robert is really worried. What will happen when she sees what life in the Hummer household is really like?

The Ghost Stallion, by Laura E. Williams. Henry Holt, 1999.

Mary Elizabeth is thirteen. In 1959 she and her father make their home with her uncle and aunt because her mother has deserted the family. Mary Elizabeth longs for some evidence of love from her father, perhaps a special name like when he calls her sister "little precious." At the same time, Pa is determined to kill a devil stallion that is luring away his horses. A stranger arrives and offers to help. As Pa, the stranger, Mary Elizabeth, and her uncle set out to find the ghost stallion, Mary Elizabeth is determined to keep the horse from being killed. In her efforts she nearly drowns, is saved by her father, and finds out the truth about her past.

More Oregon Titles

Beard, Darleen. *Operation Clean Sweep*. Farrar, Straus & Giroux, 2004.

Birdseye, Tom. *A Tough Nut to Crack*. Holiday House, 2006.

Bledsoe, Lucy. *Hoop Girls*. Holiday House, 2002.

Bunting, Eve. *The Summer of Riley*. Joanna Cotler Books, 2001.

Carey, Janet. *The Double Life of Zoe Flynn*. Atheneum, 2004.

Carlson, Melody. *Project Girl Power*. Zonderkidz, 2007.

Duey, Kathleen. *Katy and the Mustang: Book Two*. Dutton, 2004.

Gregory, Kristiana. *Seeds of Hope*. Scholastic, 2001.

Hermes, Patricia. *Across the Wide and Lonesome Prairie*. Scholastic, 1997.

Hermes, Patricia. *A Perfect Place*. Scholastic, 2002.

Hermes, Patricia. *Westward to Home: Joshua's Journal*. Scholastic, 2001.

Hermes, Patricia. *The Wild Year*. Scholastic, 2003.

Levine, Ellen. *Journal of Jedediah Barstow*. Scholastic, 2002.

Mars, Marissa. *Rachel's Journal: The Story of a Pioneer Girl*. Harcourt, 1998.

Moeri, Louise. *The Devil in Ol' Rosie*. Atheneum, 2001.

Moeri, Louise. *Save Queen of Sheba*. Atheneum, 1994.

McDonald, Megan. *The Sisters' Club*. American Girl, 2003.

Olson, Gretchen. *Call Me Hope*. Little, Brown, 2007.

Thompson, Gary. *Our Journey West*. National Geographic, 2003.

Van Leeuwen, Jean. *Bound for Oregon*. Puffin Books, 1994.

Wilson, Laura. *How I Survived the Oregon Trail*. Beech Tree, 1999.

Pennsylvania Fact Sheet

Capital: Harrisburg

Largest City: Philadelphia

Entered the Union: December 12, 1787

Tree: Hemlock

Flower: Mountain laurel

Bird: Ruffed grouse

Rivers: Allegheny, Susquehanna, Delaware, Ohio

Nickname: Keystone State

Products: Agriculture, petroleum products, electronic goods

Major Tourist Attractions:
    Gettysburg National Military Park
    Constitution Hall in Philadelphia
    Appalachian Mountain Recreation Areas

Land Area: 46,055 square miles

Population 2006: 12,365,455

Motto: Virtue Liberty and Independence

 ## Trivia

- It was in Gettysburg that President Lincoln gave his famous address in 1863.

- The first baseball stadium was built in Pittsburgh in 1909.

- Hershey, Pennsylvania, is the chocolate capital of the world.

Pennsylvania Booktalks

Goodbye Billy Radish, by Gloria Skurzynski. Tandem Library Books, 1996.

Canaan, Pennsylvania, in 1917 is a steel mill town. Hank Kerner and Bazyli Radichevych, known as Billy Radish, are fast friends, but twelve-year-old Hank rebels against the idea that a future working in the steel mill is waiting for him. Told through a series of events with World War I in the background. Hank struggles to escape a future in the mills while Billy, a Ukrainian immigrant, finds himself caught between two worlds. The boys are fast friends, yet as Hank sees the changes taking place around him he feels that he and Billy are drifting apart. The final separation comes with Billy's death from influenza. Hank vows that he will one day become a doctor and save others from the fate of his friend.

Summer Hawk, by Deborah Savage. Houghton Mifflin, 1999.

Moving from a large city to a small town is not always easy, as Taylor finds out when her family moves to the tiny town of Hunter's Gap from Philadelphia. She dislikes her new school and longs to attend a boarding school in the city. Before definite plans are made she finds an injured hawk and connects with Rail, the class outcast and Rhiannon, the Hawk Lady, who runs a rehabilitation center for injured birds. The hawk begins to heal, and Taylor gains a new respect for the work of the Hawk Lady. Taylor's earlier desire to be a journalist is set aside as she writes from the heart about her experiences that fateful summer.

Dark Shade, by Jane Curry. Simon & Schuster, 1998.

In this time trek tale Maggie Gilmore follows her friend, Kip McLean, into the wooded mountains outside the small Pennsylvania town where they live. Kip, however, has found a way into the past, back to 1758, when British soldiers are cutting a road through the dense forest, the "Dark Shade," to attack French-held Fort Duquesne. As Maggie observes Kit, she realizes that he plans to stay in the past as part of the Lenape Tribe. At the same time she stumbles across an injured soldier. He is Scottish and dressed in the red kilt of the British army. Maggie finds food and water for the soldier as well as a map to help him avoid capture by the French. Should Maggie return to the present with or without the orphan Kit? She knows her place is not in the past, but working in her father's vet clinic. It is not an easy decision to make.

Night Journey, by Avi. HarperCollins, 2000.

The year is 1767. The American Revolution has not yet begun. Peter York has lost both of his parents, and the orphan is adopted by s strict Quaker family. Peter rebels against the restrictions placed on him and sees his chance to escape the family's hold on him by capturing two runaway indentured servants and claiming the reward for doing so. He does capture one and then realizes that the bondsman is his age. Peter understands the servant's desire for freedom. Should he help his captive escape, or be more concerned about the reward money he will receive for turning in his captive?

More Pennsylvania Titles

Ayers, Katherine. *Macaroni Boy.* Delacorte, 2003.

Ayers, Katherine. *Voices at Whisper Bend.* Pleasant Company, 1999.

Bender, Carrie. *Timber Lane Cove.* Herald Press, 2003.

Bender, Carrie. *Woodland Dell's Secret.* Herald Press, 2001.

Bradley, Kimberly. *The Weaver's Daughter.* Dell, 2000.

Carrell, Marlene. *Sweet Grass Basket* Dutton, 2005.

Easton, Richard. *A Real American.* Clarion, 2002.

Ferris, Amy. *A Greater Goode: A Novel.* Houghton Mifflin, 2002.

Fritz, Jean. *The Cabin Faced West.* Putnam, 1958. Reissued 2008.

Hughes, Pat. *The Breaker Boys.* Farrar, Straus & Giroux, 2004.

Miner, Jud. *Amos and the Wild Welshman.* Author House, 2005.

Noble, Trinka. *The Last Brother: A Civil War Tale.* Sleeping Bear Press, 2006.

Osborne, Mary Pope. *My Brother's Keeper.* Scholastic, 2000.

Pryor, Bonnie. *Thomas in Danger.* Morrow, 1999.

Sorensen, Virginia. *Miracles on Maple Hill.* Harcourt, 1984.

Staples, Suzanne. *The Green Dog: A Mostly True Story.* Farrar, Straus & Giroux, 2003.

Van, Leeuwen, Jean. *Cabin on Trouble Creek.* Dial, 2004.

Woodruff, Elvira. *Dear Austin: Letters from the Underground Railroad.* Knopf, 1998.

Capital: Providence

Largest City: Providence

Entered the Union: May 29, 1790

Tree: Red maple

Flower: Violet

Bird: Rhode Island Red Hen

Rivers: Blackstone, Providence

Nickname: Ocean State

Products: Textiles, jewelry, silverware

Major Tourist Attractions:
Cliff Walk in Newport
Block Island Recreation Area
Slater Mill (museum)

Land Area: 1,545 square miles

Population 2006: 1,076,165

Motto: Hope

Trivia

- Rhode Island was the first colony to declare its independence from England but the last of the 13 original colonies to join the Union.

- An annual jazz festival is held in Newport each year.

- Newport boasts the first circus to perform in the U.S.

Rhode Island Booktalks

Finding Providence: The Story of Roger Williams, by Avi. HarperCollins, 1997.

This easy <u>I Can Read</u> chapter book tells about the founding of Providence, Rhode Island, by Roger Williams. In 1635 Mary Williams's father Roger is found guilty of preaching that is contrary to the beliefs of those in the Massachusetts Bay Colony. He escapes from the Colony, hoping with the help of the Narraganset Indians to settle in a place where many different religious beliefs are tolerated. Although life in the wilds is difficult, he eventually sends for his family to begin a new life in a place he calls Providence.

Weetamoo, Heart of the Pocasetts, by Patricia Clark Smith. Scholastic, 2003.

In 1654 Weetamoo is a young teen and daughter of the chief of the Pocasset tribe. Weetamoo knows that one day she will be the leader of the tribe and have to deal with the white settlers (called the "Coat-Men") just as her father does. Without his knowledge, she follows him to a meeting with the settlers and becomes aware of the distrust and lack of understanding between the two very different cultures. When she reaches the age for her "coming-of-age" ceremony, which requires a sweat lodge and fasting, she sees visions of the future in which the settlers and Native Americans are in conflict. The values of her tribe are stressed and include listening to and respecting the views of the elderly, older generations living with younger generations, the value of patience, and the importance of passing on time-honored traditions.

Something Upstairs: A Tale of Ghosts, by Avi. Orchard Books, 1989.

The house in Providence, Rhode Island, was built in 1789. In the kitchen there is a door that leads to a narrow flight of stairs that go to a tiny bedroom on the upper level of the house. Anyone who spends the night in this room is likely to hear strange noises and see two hands that glow and rise from a stain on the floor, followed by a human shape, that of a slave who was murdered in the early 1800s. Twelve-year-old Kenny and his family have taken up residence in the house, and the boy encounters the ghost of Caleb, the slave. Kenny is taken back in time and told that he cannot return to the present until he solves Caleb's murder. Will Kenny ever return to the present, or will he be trapped forever in Caleb's world?

The Art of Keeping Cool, by Janet Taylor Lisle. Atheneum, 2000.

Only Robert sees the plane, but the pilot is shadowy, maybe his missing father, maybe not. Robert doesn't mention his vision to Elliot, his cousin, whom he meets when he moves from Ohio with his mother and sister to live out the war (World War II) in a cabin in Rhode Island near the home of his grandparents. Elliott can draw better than anyone Robert has ever seen. He draws likenesses of the two sixteen-inch guns installed on the coast to blast German submarines out of the water. At the same time Elliott is being taught by a German artist, Abel Hoffman. Because he spends so much time prowling the beach, Hoffman is arrested and suspected of being a spy. His release, however, means tragedy when his house is burned down by the townspeople and his death when he tries to save his paintings. This is a tale of dangers, deceptive enemies, long held secrets, and two friends who find different ways of coping with the present.

More Rhode Island Titles

Avi. *The Man Who Was Poe.* Orchard Books, 1989.

Bruchac, Joseph. *Whisper in the Dark.* HarperCollins, 2005.

Griffin, Adele. *Where I Want to Be.* Putnam, 2005.

Hood, Ann. *How I Saved My Father's Life (and Ruined Everything Else).* Scholastic, 2008.

Jaspersohn, William. *The Scrimshaw Ring.* Vermont Folklife Center, 2002.

Lisle, Janet Taylor. *The Crying Rocks.* Atheneum, 2003.

Macaulay, David. *The Mill.* Houghton Mifflin, 1983.

Metz, Melinda. *Raven's Point.* HarperCollins, 2003.

Shea, Pegi. *Tangled Threads: A Hmong Girl's Story.* Clarion, 2003.

Warner, J. F. *The Case of the Lighthouse Ghost.* Lerner, 1995.

South Carolina Fact Sheet

Capital: Columbia

Largest City: Columbia

Entered the Union: May 23, 1788

Tree: Palmetto

Flower: Yellow jessamine

Bird: Carolina wren

Rivers: Santee, Edisto, Savannah

Nickname: Palmetto State

Products: Agriculture, textiles, chemicals

Major Tourist Attractions:
Charleston Museum (oldest in the U.S.)
Fort Sumter in Charleston Harbor
Myrtle Beach Seaside Resort
Hilton Head Island

Land Area: 44,820 square miles

Population 2006: 12,440,620

Motto: While I Breathe I Hope

Trivia

- Middleton Place Plantation has the oldest landscaped gardens in the U.S.

- The peach capital of the world is Johnston, South Carolina.

- The firing on Fort Sumter, April 12, 1861, marked the beginning of the Civil War.

South Carolina Booktalks

Brooklyn Rose, by Ann Rinaldi. Harcourt, 2005.

Fifteen-year-old Rose Frampton has grown up on a plantation in Beaufort County, South Carolina. Fortunately the plantation was not destroyed during the Civil War, but by 1900, as are many Southerners, the family is hard pressed for money to pay the mortgage Rose's life is revealed in the pages of the journal she receives for her birthday. The journal entries describe daily life on the plantation, visits with friends, and most important, the arrival of Rene Dumarest, a wealthy silk merchant from New York City who falls in love with Rose. For her family's sake she agrees to marry Rene and embarks on a very different life as mistress of a New York City mansion. Just as she begins to accept her new role, Rene's mother arrives and challenges Rose's ability to stand up for herself and be the true mistress of the mansion. Will Rose be up to the challenge?

Taking Care of Moses, by Barbara O'Connor. Farrar, Straus & Giroux, 2004.

Randall was supposed to go straight home after having dinner at his friend, Jaybird's, house. But on his way he sees the elderly Queenie Avery, who seems to be lost. Townsfolk of Foley, South Carolina, say she is getting more and more forgetful and should be put away in a home. Randall knows that if this happens, her husband will not want to live without her, so he follows her to keep her safe. But what does he see but a woman leaving a baby on the steps of the Rock of Ages Baptist Church? When the baby is found the townsfolk can't agree on what should be done. Should the preacher and his wife care for the child, or should it go to Miss Frieda, who provides foster care for African American children. Only Randall knows who the real mother is. Should he tell? If he reveals that he was following the lost Miss Queenie, she might be sent away. What should Randall do?

Before the Creeks Ran Red, by Carolyn Reeder. HarperCollins, 2003.

Through the eyes of three boys—Timothy, Joseph, and Gregory—three stories are told that reveal disturbing times, beginning with the secession of South Carolina and leading up to the first major battle of the Civil War. Timothy is a bugler at Fort Sumter, about to be bombarded by rebel troops. Those in the fort are on near starvation rations, and Timothy questions giving his life for his country. Both Joseph and Gregory are pulled in two directions as their families have divided loyalties. Joseph's family is staunchly Union, whereas his classmates and his best friend are for the South. Gregory's father, a Union man, disinherits Gregory's brother, who is loyal to the South. The boys' stories reveal a time in U.S. history when brother fought brother and many families had divided loyalties.

Camp of the Angel, by Aileen Arrington. Philomel, 2003.

Jordan is eleven. Her mother is in an asylum. Her father is a mean drunk, out of work more often than not, who beats her and her little brother. Jordan lies at school about her frequent bruises. Sometimes she can predict her father's anger that leads to the beatings; other times she cannot. Over time Jordan realizes that to get money, instead of working, her father is involved in criminal activities. The one thing Jordan loves other than her brother is a stray white cat. She befriends the cat and cares for it. While Jordan wonders if some of the beatings she receives are her fault, she knows that the cat is not at fault when her father deliberately hurts it. Jordan takes action and reports to the police an impending robbery in which her father will take part. Jordan and her brother eventually find a better life and hope that they may one day be reunited with their mother.

More South Carolina Titles

Clinton, Cathryn. *The Calling.* Candlewick, 2001.

Curtis, Alice. *A Yankee Girl at Fort Sumter.* Applewood, 1999.

Flood, Pansie. *Secret Holes.* Carolrhoda, 2003.

Flood, Pansie. *Sometimey Friend.* Carolrhoda, 2005.

Fuqua, Jonathon. *Darby.* Candlewick, 2002.

Hansen, Joyce. *The Heart Calls Home.* Walker, 1999.

Karr, Kathleen. *Spy in the Sky.* Hyperion, 1997.

Karr, Kathleen. *Worlds Apart.* Marshall Cavendish, 2005.

Lawler, Laurie. *Wind on the River.* Jamestown, 2000.

Luddy, Karon. *Spelldown.* Simon & Schuster, 2007.

McGill, Alice. *Miles' Song.* Houghton Mifflin, 2000.

Myers, Anna. *The Keeping Room.* Walker, 1997.

Richardson, Sandy. *The Girl Who Ate Chicken Feet.* Dial, 1998.

Rinaldi, Ann. *Cast Two Shadows: The American Revolution in the South.* Harcourt, 1998.

Rue, Nancy. *The Escape.* Bethany House, 1998.

Warner, Gertrude Chandler. *Hurricane Mystery.* Whitman, 1996.

Weston, Elise. *The Coastwatcher.* Peachtree, 2005.

Wilson, John. *The Flags of War.* Kids Can Press, 2004.

Wisler, G. Clifton. *King's Mountain.* HarperCollins, 2002.

South Dakota Fact Sheet

Capital: Pierre

Largest City: Sioux Falls

Entered the Union: November 2, 1889

Tree: Black Hills Spruce

Flower: American pasqueflower

Bird: Ring-necked pheasant

Rivers: Cheyenne, White, Missouri

Nickname: Mount Rushmore State

Products: Agriculture, cattle farming, meat products

Major Tourist Attractions:
Badlands National Park
Custer State Park
Mount Rushmore National Memorial

Land Area: 77,116 square miles

Population 2006: 6,038,403

Motto: Under God the People Rule

Trivia

- 10,000-year-old mammoth bones can be seen in Hot Springs.

- Bison roam in the wild at Custer State Park.

From *Reading the Fifty States: Booktalks, Response Activities, and More*
by Nancy Polette. Westport, CT: Libraries Unlimited. Copyright © 2009.

South Dakota Booktalks

Prairie Summer, by Arthur Geisert. Houghton Mifflin, 2002.

Farm life in the 1950s in Cresbard, South Dakota, means endless hard work for ten-year-old Rachel and her sisters. It means feeding the animals, fixing fences, stacking hay, and countless other chores. Father is a hard taskmaster, and no matter how hard Rachel tries she cannot please him. The story opens with Rachel and her sisters trying to control a herd of cattle running through a fence. Rachel is afraid of the wild Montana Angus cattle, but despite her fear tries to do all that is expected of her. She doesn't understand why her father is not as hard on her other sisters as he is on her. Then the time comes when mother is expecting a baby, and Rachel is the only one there to help. Will the early arrival of her baby brother prove that Rachel can be both competent and dependable? Will she, in her family's eyes, be able to respond to the emergency to bring about a happy outcome?

Prairie Whispers, by Frances Arrington. Philomel, 2003.

Life was hard in the 1860s on the Dakota prairie. Colleen is called upon to help her mother deliver a baby long before its time. The neighbors are too far away, and Colleen's father is away. The baby dies, and as Colleen makes her way to the neighbor's she comes across a covered wagon with a woman who has just given birth and dies after asking Colleen to look after the baby girl. In addition to the baby the woman has Colleen take her money and a gold watch. A series of events prevent Colleen from telling the truth. Then the baby's real father (a dangerous man) returns, and Colleen must make a difficult decision.

Wind on the River, by Laurie Lawlor. Jamestown, 2000.

Whose side is he on? Private John Griffith Allen, better known as Griff, is captured by Union soldiers and sent to a prison camp. It is 1863, and conditions in the camp called Point Lookout are so bad that its nickname is "death trap." Griff seizes the opportunity he is given to change sides in order to leave the camp. He agrees to fight for the Union and is sent to Fort Rice in the Dakota territory. There he finds himself in the middle of a war with Native Americans. At the same time gold has been discovered, and some men are getting very rich. Should Griff desert the army and head for the gold fields? Only he can decide what to do.

A Year Without Rain, by D. Anne Love. Holiday House, 2000.

Rachel is twelve, her brother is nine. They live on a Dakota farm in 1896 with their father. Mother died four years earlier. Work on the farm is hard, and a drought means all the work has been for nothing. Without water the crops won't grow. Father sends the two children to Atlanta to live with their aunt. There they find their mother's old trunk, with letters in it. Then father arrives to take the children home but announces also that he is to marry Miss Burke, a schoolteacher. Rachel is unhappy with the thought of her father's marriage and comes up with a plan to drive the woman away. Will she be successful, or will Rachel come to realize that a new mother is what the family needs?

More South Dakota Titles

Armstrong, Jennifer. *Black-eyed Susan.* Crown, 1995.

Bruchac, Joseph. *A Boy Called Slow.* Philomel, 1994.

Dexter, Catherine. *Driving Lessons.* Candlewick, 2000.

Hill, Pamela. *Ghost Horses.* Holiday House, 1996.

Karr, Kathleen. *The Cave.* Farrar, Straus & Giroux, 1994.

Turner, Ann. *Grasshopper Summer.* Macmillan, 1989.

Wilder, Laura Ingalls. *By the Shores of Silver Lake.* Harper & Row, 1971.

Wilder, Laura Ingalls. *The First Four Years.* Harper & Row, 1971.

Wilder, Laura Ingalls. *Little Town on the Prairie.* Harper & Row, 1972.

Wilder, Laura Ingalls. *The Long Winter.* Harper & Row, 1981.

Wilder, Laura Ingalls. *These Happy Golden Years.* Harper & Row, 1981.

Tennessee Fact Sheet

Capital: Nashville

Largest City: Memphis

Entered the Union: June 1, 1796

Tree: Tulip poplar

Flower: Iris

Bird: Mockingbird

Rivers: Tennessee, Mississippi

Nickname: Volunteer State

Products: Agriculture, automobiles

Major Tourist Attractions:
Grand Ole Opry near Nashville
Cumberland Gap National Park
The Hermitage (Home of President Andrew Jackson)
Graceland (former home of Elvis Presley)

Land Area: 42,145 square miles

Population 2006: 5,850,750

Motto: Agriculture and Commerce

 ## Trivia

- Tennessee is bordered by eight other states.

- Oak Ridge produced uranium for the first atomic weapons.

- Reelfoot Lake was formed by an earthquake that caused the Mississippi River to run backward.

Tennessee Booktalks

Swamp Angel, by Anne Isaacs. Illustrated by Paul O. Zelinsky. Dutton, 1994.

When Angelica Longrider was born, she was scarcely taller than her mother and couldn't climb a tree without help. She was a full two years old before she built her first log cabin. But by the time she is fully grown, Swamp Angel, as she is known, can lasso a tornado and drink an entire lake dry. She single-handedly saves the settlers from the fearsome bear known as Thundering Tarnation, wrestling him from the top of the Great Smoky Mountains to the bottom of a deep lake. The fight lasts five days. When both Swamp Angel and the bear are too tired to fight, they go to sleep, and Swamp Angel's snores are so loud that she snores down a huge tree, which lands on the bear and kills it. Swamp angel pays tribute to her foe and then has enough bear meat to feed everyone in Tennessee.

Come Sing Jimmy Jo, by Katherine Paterson. Dutton, 1985.

Eleven-year-old James Johnson is the son in a musical family. He has a fine voice but is shy and only sings for his grandma and occasionally with the family. On one of these occasions an agent hears James sing and insists the family take him with them for their next singing engagement. Grandma tells the boy he has a gift and must go. Little by little James overcomes his stage fright and begins to like singing for an audience as much as they like listening to him. His mother begins to resent the attention he takes from her, and family relations become more strained. How James copes with being a celebrity and keeping the family together makes a touching story.

Abby Takes a Stand, by Patricia McKissack. Viking, 2005.

Why has their grandmother bothered keeping a menu from a restaurant that closed years ago, a restaurant that never served very good food in the first place? Three cousins listen to Gee's own story, set in the early days of lunch counter sit-ins in Nashville, a time when a black child could sit up front in a city bus but still could not get a milkshake at a downtown restaurant. Through the eyes of ten-year-old Abby, young readers see what it was like to live through those days, and they'll come to understand that, like a menu, freedom is about having choices.

The Legend of Zoey: A Novel, by Candie Moonshower. Delacorte, 2006.

In this blend of fact and fantasy, thirteen-year-old Zoey places no value on her Native American heritage and is, in fact, embarrassed by it. On a field trip to Reelfoot Lake, a lightning strike causes Zoey to time trek back to 1811 when a series of severe earthquakes caused the lake to form. She meets a young girl her age, Prudence, and in journal entries from each girl the reader will experience the challenges Zoey must meet, and her growing appreciation for the past and for the connections she makes in Prudence's world.

More Tennessee Titles

Barrett, Tracy. *Cold in Summer.* Holt, 2003.

Bender, Carrie. *Timber Lane Cove.* Herald Press, 2003.

Bradley, Kimberly. *The Weaver's Daughter.* Delacorte, 2000.

Christvans, Craig. *Moon Over Tennessee.* Houghton Mifflin, 1999

Dowell, Frances. *Where I'd Like to Be.* Atheneum, 2003.

Ernst, Kathleen. *Hearts of Stone.* Dutton, 2006.

Hermes, Patricia. *Sweet By and By.* HarperCollins, 2002.

Johnston, Tony. *Bone by Bone.* Roaring Brook Press, 2007.

Keehn, Sally. *Gnat Stokes and the Foggy Bottom Swamp Queen.* Philomel, 2005.

McKissack, Patricia. *Color Me Dark.* Scholastic, 2000.

McKissack, Patricia. *A Song for Harlem.* Viking, 2007.

McKissack, Patricia *Tippy Lemmey.* Aladdin, 2003.

Murphy, Rita. *Harmony.* Delacorte, 2002.

Myers, Anna. *Graveyard Girl.* Walker, 1995.

Partridge, Elizabeth. *Clara and the Hoodoo Man.* Dutton, 1996.

Schwabach, Karen. *The Hope Chest.* Random House, 2008.

Sobol, Donald. *Encyclopedia Brown Shows the Way.* Dell Yearling, 2003.

Steele, William O. *The Perilous Road.* Harcourt, 1990.

Wisler, G. Clifton. *Buffalo Moon.* Dutton, 1984.

Wisler, G. Clifton. *Jericho's Journey.* Dutton, 1989.

Wisler, G. Clifton. *Thunder on the Tennessee.* Dutton, 1983.

Capital: Austin

Largest City: Houston

Entered the Union: December 29, 1845

Tree: Pecan

Flower: Bluebonnet

Bird: Mockingbird

Rivers: Brazos, Red, Rio Grande

Nickname: Lone Star State

Products: Petroleum, natural gas, livestock, cotton

Major Tourist Attractions:
  The Alamo in San Antonio
  The Lyndon B. Johnson Space Center
  Big Bend National Park
  The Science Place and Dallas Museum of Natural History

Land Area: 261,915 square miles

Population 2006: 23,500,800

Motto: Friendship

Trivia

- Six flags have flown over Texas since 1519.

- Texas is the second largest state.

- Houston is the home of NASA, headquarters for space flights.

Texas Booktalks

A Paradise Called Texas, by Janice Jordan Shefelman. Eakin Press, 1983.

Searching for a better life, Mina, Papa, and Mama left their German fatherland aboard the brig *Margaretha*, bound for Texas. They had been told it was the paradise of North America, but when Mina steps onto the desolate beach at Indian Point on a cold December day in 1845, she wants to go back to Germany and Opa's cozy house in the village of Wehrstedt.

But go on they must. In spite of Mama's tragic death, Mina and Papa push inland with the Kaufmann family to the Texas hill country. There Mina encounters an Indian chief and his young daughter, Amaya, whose help she needs when Papa falls ill.

Based on her ancestors' immigration to Texas, the author tells about a journey into the wilderness that is filled with hardship, tragedy, and adventure.

Holes, by Louis Sachar. Farrar, Straus & Giroux, 1998.

Stanley Yelnat's family has a history of bad luck, so he isn't too surprised when a miscarriage of justice sends him to a boy's juvenile detention center., Camp Green Lake. The camp is located in a barren region of Texas, a hundred miles from the nearest water source. Water is brought in by truck. Among dangers the boys face are rattlers, scorpions, and yellow-spotted lizards. There is no lake, it has been dry for over a hundred years, and it's hardly a camp: as punishment, the boys must each dig a hole a day, five feet deep, five feet across, in the hard earth of the dried-up lake bed. The warden claims that this pointless behavior builds character, but that's a lie. Stanley must try to dig up the truth.

When Zachary Beaver Came to Town, by Kimberly Willis Holt. Dell Yearling, 1999.

Three boys are central to this novel. Toby and Cal are best friends. Toby's mother has gone to Nashville to pursue a singing career. Cal's brother, Wayne, is fighting in Vietnam. Cal's dad has a cotton farm, and the boys look forward to the annual ladybug waltz, when sacks of ladybugs are set free over the farm and Toby's father plays classical music. The third boy in the tale is Zachary Beaver, who arrives in a trailer as "The Fattest Boy in the World." People pay admission to see him and hear his wild tales, until the man who brought him disappears. Zachary has a dream that he fears will never be realized, until Toby and Cal be-friend him. With some difficulty the boys help Zachary. When his guardian finally returns to take Zachary away, Toby and Cal are glad that Zachary Beaver came to town.

Come Juneteenth, by Ann Rinaldi. Harcourt, 2007.

Sis Goose is a beloved member of Luli's family, despite the fact that she was born a slave. But the family is harboring a terrible secret. And when Union soldiers arrive on their Texas plantation to announce that slaves have been declared free for nearly two years, Sis Goose is horrified to find that the people she called family have lied to her for so long. She runs away, but her newly found freedom has tragic consequences.

How could the state of Texas keep the news of the Emancipation Proclamation from reaching slaves? Here are the events that led to the creation of Juneteenth, a celebration of freedom that continues today.

More Texas Titles

Burks, Brian. *Wrango.* Harcourt, 1999.

Erickson, John. *Discovery at Flint Springs.* Viking, 2004.

Erickson, John. *Moonshiner's Gold.* Viking, 2001.

Ford, Christine. *Scout.* Delacorte, 2006.

Garland, Sherry. *A Line in the Sand.* Scholastic, 1998.

Gipson, Fred. *Old Yeller.* HarperCollins, 1956. Reissued 2006.

Gipson, Fred. *Savage Sam.* HarperCollins, 1958.

Griffin, Penny. *The Music Thief.* Holt, 2002.

Griffin, Penny. *Switching Well.* Macmillan, 1993.

Holt, Kimberly. *Dancing in Cadillac Light.* Puffin Books, 2001.

Hunt, Laura. *The Abernathy Boys.* HarperCollins, 2004.

Ibbotson, Eva. *Haunting of Granite Falls.* Dutton, 2004.

Jackson, Louise. *Gone to Texas.* Eakin, 2004.

Janke, Katelan. *Survival in the Storm.* Scholastic, 2002.

Lasky, Katherine. *Christmas After All.* Scholastic, 2001.

Love, Anne. *1 Remember the Alamo.* Holiday House, 1999.

Nixon, Joan Lowry. *David's Search.* Delacorte, 1998.

Nixon, Joan Lowry. *Search for the Shadowman.* Scholastic, 1996.

Saunders, Susan. *Lucky Lady.* HarperCollins, 2000.

Snyder, Zilpha Keatley. *Cat Running.* Delacorte, 1996.

Wisler, G. Clifton. *Cobb's Choice.* Dutton, 1996.

Wisler, G. Clifton. *Jericho's Journey.* Dutton, 1993.

Utah Fact Sheet

Capital: Salt Lake City

Largest City: Salt Lake City

Entered the Union: January 4, 1896

Tree: Blue Spruce

Flower: Sego lily

Bird: California gull

Rivers: Colorado, Green

Nickname: Beehive State

Products: Oil, coal copper, iron ore, gold, silver cattle

Major Tourist Attractions:
Bryce Canyon National Park
Monument Valley
Great Salt Lake
Newspaper Rock Historical Monument

Land Area: 84,900 square miles

Population 2006: 2,350,450

Motto: Industry

Trivia

- The transcontinental railroad was completed in 1869, when east and west crews met at Promontory Point, Utah.

- Four states—Arizona, Colorado, New Mexico, and Utah—all meet at Four Corners.

- The Mormon Temple in Salt Lake City took 40 years to complete.

Utah Booktalks

The Great Brain, by John D. Fitzgerald. Doubleday, 1967.

The Great Brain of Adenville, Utah, is Tom. His great brain is always at work, outwitting his friends, his family, the citizens of Adenville, and even the Adenville School Board. Tom saves the Jensen brothers from death, fights the meanest bullies, and is always looking for a way to make a profit. When Mr. Standish, the mean school master, crosses the Great Brain, Tom puts his mind to work to devise a devilish scheme. The results are surprising.

The Great Brain always seems to come out on top, and more important, makes a profit. Will the Great Brain ever truly reform? Do his schemes go too far? The excitement and surprises continue as the Great Brain gets older and moves to the Catholic Academy in Salt Lake City. You can find more surprising and funny stories about the Great Brain's adventures by reading the series of books by John D. Fitzgerald. The stories are based on his life in Utah and his adventures with his brother, Tom, who was always making mischief.

Ghost Horses, by Gloria Skurzynski. National Geographic, 2000.

Jack Landon, thirteen, and his sister Ashley, ten, arrive at Zion National Park with their parents and two foster Native American children, Ethan and Summer. Jack's mother is a wildlife biologist who is investigating the deaths of wild horses in the park. Ethan resents being with the family and constantly complains. Summer seems to have information about the horses. Is Ethan behind the accidents that happen? Will the hike through the Narrows prove to be life threatening? Are stampeding horses and falling rocks the result of a Ghost Dance Ethan teaches Jack and Ashley, or are more dangerous forces at work?

Bearstone, by Will Hobbs. Macmillan, 1989.

Cloyd pulled the blue stone from his pocket and set the little bear on a flat rock at the very top of the mountain. "Lone Bear," he said aloud, "we're not so alone anymore."

Cloyd hasn't gone to school in four years. He has grown up without his parents, half-wild and alone, leading his grandmother's goats into remote Utah canyons. Sent away by his tribe to a group home in Colorado, he fails in school and runs away in search of his father, whom he has never known. Disappointed, he returns to the group home, alone.

When summer comes, Cloyd is sent to work for an old rancher, who tells fascinating tales about a gold mine in the nearby mountains. Above the ranch, Cloyd finds a small turquoise bear and forges a new identity as "Lone Bear." He battles the old man over the never-ending ranch work, longs to ride off to the mountains, and makes an enemy of a bear hunter he will meet again. Finally reconciled, Cloyd and the old man ride into the high country together.

The Maze, by Will Hobbs. HarperCollins, 1999.

Wandering alone in the Maze in Canyonlands National Park is not a good idea. Fourteen-year-old Rick Walker, who is on the run from the law, is fortunate to encounter Lon, a man with a mission. Lon, a bird biologist, tracks and feeds condors to release them back into the wild. Rick and Lon strike up a friendship, and Lon teaches Rick hang gliding. Rick, in turn, trusts Lon enough to tell him about his past. Two unsavory characters hiding weapons in the area mean danger to Rick and Lon, and Rick risks his life to save his new friend. This is an exciting, action-packed tale as a young boy finds his way out of trouble.

More Utah Titles

Cushman, Karen. *Rodzina.* Clarion, 2003.

Fitzgerald, John. *More Adventures of the Great Brain.* Dial, 1969.

Fitzgerald, John. *Return of the Great Brain.* Dial, 1974.

Gregory, Kristiana. *The Great Railroad Race.* Scholastic, 1999.

Harrison, Mette. *The Monster in Me.* Holiday House, 2003.

Hulme, Joy. *Through the Open Door.* HarperCollins, 2000.

Jones, Marcia. *Ghostville Elementary, Frights, Camera, Action!* Scholastic, 2005.

Litchman, Kristen. *All Is Well.* Delacorte, 1998.

Myers, Edward. *Hostage.* Hyperion, 1996.

Skurzynski, Gloria. *Rockbuster.* National Geographic, 2004.

Uchida, Yoshiko. *Journey to Topaz: A Story of the Japanese-American Evacuation.* Scribner, 1971.

Wunderli, Stephen. *The Blue Between the Clouds.* Holt, 1992.

Vermont Fact Sheet

Capital: Montpelier

Largest City: Burlington

Entered the Union: March 4, 1791

Tree: Sugar maple

Flower: Red clover

Bird: Hermit thrush

Rivers: Connecticut, West, Otter

Nickname: Green Mountain State

Products: Dairy products, paper

Major Tourist Attractions:
Green Mountains recreation areas
St. Albans Maple Festival
Shelburne Museum

Land Area: 9,615 square miles

Population 2006: 620,110

Motto: Freedom and Unity

 ## Trivia

- Two-thirds of Vermont's population live in the country.

- Vermont was the first state to join the Union after the original thirteen.

- Vermont produces more maple syrup than any other state.

Vermont Booktalks

Snowflake Bentley, by Jacqueline Briggs Martin. Illustrated by Mary Azarian. Houghton Mifflin, 1998

Snow in Vermont is as common as dirt. Why would anyone want to photograph it? But from the time he was a small boy, Wilson Bentley thought of the icy crystals as small miracles, and he determines that one day his camera will capture for others their extraordinary beauty. Often misunderstood in his time, Wilson Bentley took pictures that even today reveal two important truths about snowflakes: First, that no two are alike, and second, that each one is startlingly beautiful. Here is the story of a simple farmer who had not only a scientist's vision and perseverance, but also a clear passion for the wonders of nature.

Rabbit Hill, by Robert Lawson. Viking Press, 1944.

The story opens with excitement because New Folks are moving into the big house that borders the hill. Little Georgie Rabbit ventures off into the countryside to fetch his Uncle Analdas to stay with them. He has quite an adventure along the way. When the New Folks arrive, all the animals watch in apprehension, wondering if the folks are good or bad. They scrutinize the people's belongings looking for traps, snares, spring-guns, poison, dogs, or cats. Finding only a cat, Mr. Muldoon, who proves to be harmless, the animals are relieved. Their excitement mounts as large garden and buckwheat fields are planted. Other evidence proving the New Folks are friendly appears. The climax comes when Little Georgie, everyone's favorite little rabbit, is hit by the man's car. Georgie is taken inside the big house and not heard from again. Everyone is troubled and angered over Georgie. A large covered box appears on the little lawn under the pine tree. When it is unveiled all of the animals are present. What can it be? Does it have something to do with Little Georgie?

Kitty and Mr. Kipling: Neighbors in Vermont, by Lenore Blegvad. Atheneum, 2005.

In 1892 world-famous English author Rudyard Kipling and his wife come to live in Dummerston, Vermont, and everything changes for young Kitty, who lives on a neighboring farm. Kitty is curious about and fascinated by the Kiplings. She realizes at once that she has never met—nor will she ever again meet—as interesting a man as Rudyard Kipling. He's full of spectacular stories of drama and adventure. He tells her all about India (a place beyond Kitty's wildest dreams!) and reads to her from a new story he is writing about a boy named Mowgli, who lives with wolves in the jungle. Imagine! Kitty, in turn, teaches the remarkable Mr. Kipling the strange ways of Vermonters and helps with the Kiplings' new baby. In Kitty's own house her parents are constantly telling her that "curiosity killed the cat," but in Mr. Kipling's company the world seems wide open for Kitty to explore. However, as she soon discovers, not everyone is as happy with the Kiplings' move to Kitty's town as she is, and she comes to understand that the uncovering and acceptance of truths can be a painful process.

Taking Wing, by Nancy Graff. Clarion, 2005.

Wartime in rural Vermont in (1942) means rationing, victory gardens, and watching for enemy planes. Gus is sent to live with his grandparents on their Vermont farm while his father is in pilot training and his mother is ill. He finds abandoned duck eggs and is determined to care for the newly hatched ducklings.

A strange young girl arrives and wants to help. Her name is Louise. The town and Gus's grandparents shun the child and her family. They are poor and from Quebec. Gus learns not only about prejudice but also about loss, as all but one of the ducklings dies, and that one must be freed. He makes mistakes in trying to help Louise and must take action to keep her friendship.

More Vermont Titles

Anderson, M. T. *The Game of Sunken Places.* Scholastic, 2004.

Doyle, Eugenie. *Stray Voltage.* Front Street, 2002.

Gauch, Patricia. *Aaron and the Green Mountain Boys.* Boyds Mills, 1972. Reissued 2005.

Gauthier, Gail. *The Hero of Ticonderoga.* Putnam, 2001.

Gorden, Nancy. *Case of the Golden Scarab.* Two Lies Publishing, 2004.

Graff, Nancy. *A Long Way Home.* Clarion, 2001.

Hahn, Mary Downing. *All the Lovely Bad Ones: A Ghost Story.* Clarion, 2008.

Henry, Marguerite. *Justin Morgan Had a Horse.* Simon & Schuster, 1982.

Hurwitz, Johanna. *Dear Emma.* HarperCollins, 2002.

Hurwitz, Johanna. *Faraway Summer.* Morrow, 1998.

Ketchum, Liza. *Where the Great Hawk Flies.* Clarion, 2005.

Kinsey-Warnock, Natalie. *A Doctor Like Papa.* HarperCollins, 2002.

Maguire, Jerry. *A Couple of April Fools.* Clarion, 2004.

Maguire, Jerry. *One Final Firecracker.* Clarion, 2005.

Maguire, Jerry. *Three Rotten Eggs.* Clarion, 2002.

Paterson, Katherine. *The Field of the Dogs.* HarperCollins, 2001.

Paterson, Katherine. *Jip, His Story.* Dutton, 1996.

Peck, Robert Newton. *Soup.* Dell Yearling, 1998.

Rupp, Rebecca. *Sarah Simpson's Rules for Living.* Candlewick Press, 2008.

Seidler, Tor. *Brothers Below Zero.* Laura Geringer Books, 2002.

Winthrop, Elizabeth. *Counting on Grace.* Wendy Lamb Books, 2006.

Virginia Fact Sheet

Capital: Richmond

Largest City: Virginia Beach

Entered the Union: June 25, 1788

Tree: Dogwood

Flower: American dogwood

Bird: Cardinal

Rivers: James, Rappahannock, Potomac, Shenandoah

Nicknames: The Old Dominion and Mother of Presidents

Products: Agriculture, coal, lumber, furniture

Major Tourist Attractions:
James Fort in Jamestown
Mount Vernon, home of George Washington
Monticello, home of Thomas Jefferson
Williamsburg

Land Area: 42,775 square miles

Population 2006: 7,780,340

Motto: Thus Always to Tyrants

Trivia

- Jamestown was the first permanent English settlement in America.

- Richmond was the capital of the Confederate States of America in the Civil War.

- More U.S. presidents were born in Virginia than any other state.

Virginia Booktalks

Charley Skedaddle, by Patricia Beatty. William Morrow, 1987.

Charley has longed to experience the glory of war and enlists in the Union army to avenge his brother's death and to escape from his previous bowery life. Too young to be a soldier, he enlists as a drummer boy. During his first battle, Charley kills a man and is so traumatized by this that he skedaddles to the mountains of Virginia. There he truly proves his courage by saving the life of suspicious Granny Bent, who makes him fetch and carry for her. When she is hurt, Charley has the courage to confront a panther and get her home safely. Surprisingly, Charley finds his courage not on the battlefield but in the mountains. He is now ready to leave the mountains, with the strong intention that one day he will return.

The Serpent Never Sleeps, by Scott O'Dell. Houghton Mifflin, 1987.

"The ring the king gave her was shaped like a serpent and it would protect her he said, even across the seas." Serena Lynn, age seventeen, is asked by England's King James I to serve at court. She is very pleased, but must decline: she is loyal to the man she has always loved, Anthony Foxcroft. Anthony is embroiled in disputes at court and must ship out for Jamestown, the first colony in the New World. Serena will go too.

They sail on the *Sea Venture,* which leaves Plymouth, England, in 1609 to take supplies and more settlers to Virginia. Their small boat seems no match for the wild sea, but they are spared—only to be shipwrecked off Bermuda. The brave crew builds a new boat so their expedition can flounder on to Virginia.

When they arrive, Jamestown is in ruins. Those who have survived the deadly winter are in desperate need of food. The Indians, with whom the colonists have maintained a delicate peace, may be their only chance. Serena goes with a party sent to plead with Pocahontas, the Indian princess who saved them once before, and who may have the power to save them again.

Shades of Gray, by Carolyn Reeder. Macmillan, 1989.

The Civil War is over, but to twelve-year-old Will Page the Yankees are still enemies. How can it be otherwise, when the war has claimed his entire immediate family? Now Will must live with relatives in the Virginia Piedmont. This would be bearable if Will's uncle had participated in the war—but Jed Jones refused to fight the Yankees.

Although bitterly resentful, Will has to accept his uncle's hospitality and share rural life, working beside him in a way no city boy has ever worked. As Will learns during the long, hot summer to trap rabbits, hoe the garden, mend the fence, and more, he comes to admire his uncle's ability to do just about anything. Still, in Will's eyes the man's skill and generosity are not enough to win respect, much less love. How will he ever manage to stay in this place?

Then an opportunity comes for Will to go home and live with a family friend. To his surprise, Will feels torn—until Uncle Jed allows a traveling Yankee to rest on his farm and reignites all of Will's rancor.

Give Me Liberty, by L. M. Elliott. HarperCollins, 2008.

Life is not easy for Nathaniel, a thirteen-year-old indentured servant in colonial Virginia. Though things improve with the help of a kind schoolmaster named Basil, who shares music, books, and philosophies on equality, the climate all around is heating up. It is 1775, and colonists are enraged by England's taxation. Soon Patrick Henry's words, "Give me liberty or give me death," become the sounding call for action. Nathaniel and Basil must decide whether to join the action as they face the larger question of the true meaning of liberty. Here is a stirring story of one boy's involvement in the American Revolution.

More Virginia Titles

Armstrong, Alan. *Raleigh's Page.* Random House, 2007.

Blume, Lesley. *Cornelia and the Audacious Escapades of the Somerset Sisters.* Dell Yearling, 2008.

Carbone, Elisa. *Night Running.* Knopf, 2008.

Dahlberg, Maureen. *The Spirit of Billy Bucket.* Farrar, 2002.

Fritz, Jean. *Who's Saying What in Jamestown, Thomas Savage?* Putnam, 2007.

Hahn, Mary Downing. *Witch Catcher.* Clarion, 2006.

Henry, Marguerite. *Misty of Chincoteague.* Aladdin Books, 1975.

Hite, Sid. *Journal of Rufus Rowe.* Scholastic, 2003.

Kudlinski, Kathleen. *My Lady Pocahontas: A Novel.* Marshall Cavendish, 2006.

Lester, Julius. *Time's Memory.* Farrar, Straus & Giroux, 2006.

Murphy, Jim. *Journal of James Edward Pease: A Civil War Union Soldier.* Scholastic, 2003.

Paterson, Katherine. *Bridge to Terabithia.* Thomas Y. Crowell, 1977.

Ransom, Candice. *Finding Day's Bottom.* Carolrhoda, 2006.

Rinaldi, Ann. *An Unlikely Friendship: A Novel of Mary Todd Lincoln and Elizabeth Keckley.* Harcourt, 2007.

Ruby, Lois. *Journey to Jamestown.* Kingfisher, 2005.

Rylant, Cynthia. *Missing May.* Scholastic, 1992.

Seabrooke, Brenda. *The Haunting of Swain's Fancy.* Dutton, 2003.

Tripp, Valerie. *Very Funny, Elizabeth.* Pleasant Company, 2005.

White, Ruth. *The Search for Belle Prater.* Farrar, Straus & Giroux, 2005.

White, Ruth. *Way Down Deep.* Farrar, Straus & Giroux, 2007.

Wilson, Douglas. *Blackthorn Winter.* Veritas Press, 2003.

Washington Fact Sheet

Capital: Olympia

Largest City: Seattle

Entered the Union: November 11, 1889

Tree: Western hemlock

Flower: Coast rhododendron

Bird: Willow goldfinch

Rivers: Columbia, Snake, Spokane

Nickname: Evergreen State

Products: Agriculture, apples, lumber, aircraft

Major Tourist Attractions:
Grand Coulee Cam
Mount Rainier
Pacific Science Center: Seattle
Mount St. Helens National Volcanic Monument
John Day Fossil Beds National Monument

Land Area: 71,300 square miles

Population 2006: 6,130,445

Motto: By and By

Trivia

- Washington is the leading apple growing state.

- Mount St. Helens erupted in 1980, killing 57 people.

- The state of Washington has had many Bigfoot sightings.

Washington Booktalks

The Ghost's Grave, by Peg Kehret. Dutton, 2005.

What Josh thought would be the dullest summer of his life, spent with his eccentric great-aunt in Carbon City, Washington, turns out to be a chilling adventure. His Aunt Ethel serves dinner for breakfast and thinks the peacock on the porch is her dead sister. Until his folks left for India, Josh had expected to spend the summer playing baseball. What Josh did not expect was to meet Willie, the ghost of a coal miner killed in a mine explosion. Willie has been waiting for years for some kind soul to dig up his leg and rebury it with the rest of him. Only then will he be at peace. Josh agrees to do the grisly deed, but when he digs in the old cemetery, he finds more than Willie's leg bones. Who buried the box of cash in the grave, and why? How far will that person go to get the money back? How can Willie, the peacock and a quick-thinking neighbor help? Find out in this spooky adventure tale.

The Grape Thief, by Kristine Franklin. Candlewick, 2003.

Slava Petrovich has a most unusual ability for a boy of twelve. He earns the nickname, Cuss, because he can curse in twelve languages. The poor coal mining town of Roslyn, Washington, in 1925 is home to immigrants from many countries. Cuss and his friends vie to see who can steal the most grapes from the grape train that comes annually from California. Instead, Cuss's older brothers become involved in a killing and must flee, leaving Cuss as the man of the family to care for his mother and sister. Cuss, who is very bright and a good student, must choose between school and earning money to help his family. How can he keep his dream to get an education yet be the wage earner for his family? Cuss has some tough decisions to make.

Our Only May Amelia, by Jennifer Holm. HarperCollins, 1999.

In 1899 along Washington's Nasel River lived a young girl with seven brothers. Not only did she have seven brothers, but May Amelia was the only girl in the community. She tagged after her brothers, and much to her parents' dismay, tried to do everything they did, including fishing, making fish nets, and yelling to the villagers when logs were coming down the river. Her parents want her to be more ladylike, which is more and more difficult for the high-spirited girl to do. She does help her mother with the chores, tends the sheep, and eagerly awaits the birth of her mother's new baby, which turns out to be a little sister. Sadly, however, the baby dies, and Amelia May runs away to live with an uncle and aunt and work through her grief. This novel is based on the real-life experiences of the author's great-aunt, the real May Amelia.

Sarah and Me and the Lady from the Sea, by Patricia Beatty. William Morrow, 1989.

The year is 1895. Twelve-year-old Marcella Abbott can't believe her family is giving up their home in Portland, Oregon, and their comfortable life in the city to go and live permanently in their beach house on Washington State's Olympic Peninsula. The family has no choice but to move because the father's business has failed. Marcella, however, is determined not to make the best of it. She thinks the people of Nahcotta are stupid, oafish country bumpkins. But three things change her mind forever: a new friend named Sarah, a beached whale, and a mysterious lady who survived a terrible storm at sea. Spend the summer with Marcella, her brother, and her sister for a highly rewarding experience.

More Washington Titles

DeGuzman, Michael. *The Bamboozlers.* Farrar, Straus & Giroux, 2005.

Frazier, Sundee. *Brendan Buckley's Universe and Everything In It.* Delacorte, 2007.

Frederick, Heather. *The Black Paw.* Simon & Schuster, 2005.

Irving, Washington. *The Legend of Sleepy Hollow.* Atheneum, 2007.

Johns, Linda. *Hannah West in Deep Water: A Mystery.* Puffin Books, 2006.

Kelly, Katy. *Lucy Rose: Big on Plans.* Delacorte, 2005.

Kelly, Katy. *Lucy Rose, Working Myself to Pieces and Bits.* Delacorte, 2007.

Kimmel, Eric. *Rip Van, Winkle's Return.* Farrar, Straus & Giroux, 2007.

Lyons, Kelly. *One Million Men and Me.* Just Us Books, 2007.

Martin, Nora. *Flight of the Fisherbird.* Bloomsbury, 2003.

Matas, Carol. *The Whirlwind,* Orca Publishers, 2007.

Monthei, Betty. *Looking for Normal.* HarperCollins, 2005.

Patneaude, David. *The Last Man's Reward.* Whitman, 1996.

Platt, Randall. *The Likes of Me.* Delacorte, 2000.

Ransom, Candice. *Rider in the Night.* Wizards of the Coast, 2007.

Roy, Ron. *Fireworks at the FBI.* Random House, 2006.

Roy, Ron. *Who Broke Lincoln's Thumb?* Random House, 2005.

Sharpe, Susan. *Spirit Quest.* Bradbury, 1991.

St. George, Judith. *The Ghost, the White House and Me.* Holiday House, 2007.

Stolls, Amy. *Palms to the Ground.* Farrar, Straus & Giroux, 2001.

Yolen, Jane. *The Wizard of Washington Square.* Starscape, 2005.

West Virginia Fact Sheet

Capital: Charleston

Largest City: Charleston

Entered the Union: June 20, 1863

Tree: Sugar maple

Flower: Rhododendron

Bird: Cardinal

Rivers: Guyandotte, Greenbriar, Ohio

Nickname: Mountain State

Products: Coal, steel, and glass products

Major Tourist Attractions:
Harpers Ferry National Historic Park
The steam-powered train at Cass
White Sulphur Springs

Land Area: 24,230 square miles

Population 2006: 1,810,350

Motto: Mountaineers Are Always Free

Trivia

- West Virginia has fewer than 20,000 farms.
- The first Mother's Day celebration took place in Grafton in 1908.
- Three-quarters of the state is forest land.

West Virginia Booktalks

Shiloh, by Phyllis Reynolds Naylor. Macmillan, 1991.

Marty lives with his family in a house in the woods of Friendly, West Virginia. Sometimes he helps his dad deliver mail; other times he spends time in the hills or walking along the creek. One day when he is walking by the gristmill near the Shiloh bridge, a dog starts following him. Marty has always wanted a dog, but because his grandma was feeble and the family had to send money to help take care of her, there was no money to feed and take care of a pet . There is something about this dog, though, like he's afraid of getting a whooping or something, so Marty acts like he doesn't see him. Starting to whistle is like pressing a magic button: the beagle come barreling toward the boy, legs going lickety-split; he licks all Marty's fingers and jumps up against his leg! When Marty gets home he finds out that Judd Travers is missing a beagle. Now, nobody likes Judd Travers; he is mean and dirty, he even hunts out of season, and doesn't treat his dogs right. Marty doesn't want his new-found dog to have to go back to Judd Travers, so he builds a lean-to to keep the dog dry when it rains and is determined to keep his new pet a secret from his family.

Billy Creekmore, by Tracey Porter. HarperCollins, 2007.

Billy Creekmore knows nothing about his parents except for picture postcards from his father and tales of his mother's death during childbirth. In the early 1900s Billy is growing up in the cruel clutches of the Guardian Angels Home for Boys. Billy longs to escape. When a stranger comes to claim him, Billy sets off on an incredible adventure, from the coal mines of West Virginia to the spectacular world of a traveling circus. Faced with an uncertain future and a mysterious past, Billy's extraordinary journey is one of survival, truth, and ultimately, hope.

Missing May, by Cynthia Rylant. Orchard, 1992.

Ever since six-year-old Summer became an orphan, she has been passed from relative to relative. Finally she ends up in the care of Uncle Ob and Aunt May. These two older adults don't have much to give Summer except endless love. But the loving family is not to stay together for long, for Aunt May dies. Ob is torn with grief and doesn't think he can go on. Then Summer and Ob meet Cletus, a teenager, who claims he has had an afterlife experience and convinces them he knows a person who can help them contact May.

In their grief both Ob and Summer seek out the spiritualist, but they are destined to have their hopes shattered. Eventually the two are able to accept May's death. With the coming of spring they put whirligigs in May's garden and dedicate them to her.

Shadows, by Dennis Haseley. Farrar, Straus & Giroux, 1991.

While his widowed mother is looking for work, Jamie is spending the summer in rural West Virginia with his aunt and uncle. The lonely boy finds company when grandpa comes to visit and shows the boy how to make shadow pictures on the wall. Grandpa also tells the boy many heroic tales about his father, who was killed in a factory accident. Jamie's aunt disapproves of grandpa's visits, knowing that Jamie's father was inclined to recklessness rather than heroics. One sleepless night the shadows beckon Jamie to grandpa's cabin, where the boy rescues the old man from a room filled with smoke. When Jamie's mother finds a job and comes to get him, the boy leaves a summer experience believing that some things about his father must be true, just as the shadows came alive to lead Jamie out into the night to Grandpa's cabin.

More West Virginia Titles

Anderson, Jade. *May Bird Among the Stars.* Atheneum, 2006.

Baker, Julie. *Up Molasses Mountain.* Wendy Lamb Books, 2002.

Belton, Sandra. *McKendree.* Greenwillow, 2000.

Bowdish, Lynea. *Brooklyn, Bugsy and Me.* Farrar, Straus & Giroux, 2000.

Cabot, Meg. *Project Princess.* HarperCollins, 2003.

Cushman, Karen. *Rodzina.* Clarion, 2003.

Durant, Lynda. *Betsy Zane, the Rose of Fort Henry.* Clarion, 2000.

Hahn, Mary D. *Witch Catcher.* Clarion, 2006.

High, Linda. *Hound Heaven.* Holiday House, 1995.

Naylor, Phyllis Reynolds. *Girls Rule.* Delacorte, 2004.

Naylor, Phyllis Reynolds. *Saving Shiloh.* Atheneum, 1997.

Naylor, Phyllis Reynolds. *Shiloh Season.* Atheneum, 1996.

Rinaldi, Ann. *The Coffin Quilt: The Feud Between the Hatfields and the McCoys.* Harcourt, 1999.

Rylant, Cynthia. *Blue Eyed Daisy.* Bradbury, 1985.

Seabrooke, Brenda. *The Haunting of Swain's Fancy.* Dutton, 2003.

Seely, Debra. *Grasslands.* Holiday House, 2002.

White, Ruth. *Way Down Deep.* Farrar, Straus & Giroux, 2007.

Yep, Laurence. *Dream Soul.* HarperCollins, 2000.

Wisconsin Fact Sheet

Capital: Madison

Largest City: Milwaukee

Entered the Union: May 29, 1848

Tree: Sugar maple

Flower: Wood violet

Bird: Robin

Rivers: Chippewa, Mississippi, Wisconsin

Nickname: Badger State

Products: Dairy products, paper products, beer

Major Tourist Attractions:
Milwaukee Public Museum
Wisconsin Dells
Circus World Museum in Baraboo

Land Area: 65,500 square miles

Population 2006: 5,500,300

Motto: Forward

Trivia

- Wisconsin leads the nation in production of milk, butter,and cheese.

- French explorers were the first Europeans to set foot in Wisconsin, in the 1600s.

- More than 200 tops are on display at the Spinning Top Museum in Burlington.

Wisconsin Booktalks

Caddie Woodlawn, by Carol Ryrie Brink. Little, Brown, 1976.

In 1864 on the Wisconsin frontier it is hard to tell which of the Woodlawn family were boys. The Wisconsin territory can be a rugged and dangerous place, but for Caddie Woodlawn it is beautiful and ripe for adventure. Caddie an run and jump and climb trees as easily as her brothers Tom and Warren, and much to the dismay of her mother and sister, Clara. She detests frilly clothes, walking, or sitting in lady-like fashion, and most of all the thought that her mother and others expect her to behave in a proper manner. But because of Caddie's adventurous spirit, a disaster is averted with the neighboring Indian tribe, with whose leader, Indian John, Caddie has become friends. Here is a tale of pioneer life as it was lived and of a spirited young girl whose parents despair of her ever becoming ladylike.

Little House in the Big Woods, by Laura Ingalls Wilder. HarperCollins, 1954.

The <u>Little House</u> books tell the story of Laura Ingalls Wilder's life. She was born in 1867 in a little log cabin on the edge of the Big Woods of Wisconsin, and through the years she traveled with her family by covered wagon through Kansas, Minnesota, and finally the Dakota Territory, where she met and married Almanzo Wilder.

There was deprivation and hard work. Crops were ruined by storms and grasshopper plagues. But there were also the happy times of love and laughter: sleigh rides, holiday celebrations, and socials that bring the Ingalls family vividly alive and capture the best of the American pioneer spirit.

Rascal, by Sterling North. Dutton, 1963.

Many young boys have a dog as their constant companion. Eleven-year-old Sterling North has a raccoon named Rascal. Rascal and Sterling do everything together—from winning a pie-eating contest to fishing for trout in the Wisconsin forests.

It would have been perfect—if only Rascal weren't so clever. The day comes when Rascal is too smart for his own good. Sterling must make a difficult choice—either cage his beloved raccoon or take him away and let him go free.

Sterling North was born in Wisconsin in 1906 and died in 1974. He was raised by his father on a farm. His mother died when he was a young boy, and he was often alone. He had many pets for company, and *Rascal* is the true story of Sterling and his animals, which included not only the raccoon, but a Saint Bernard, several cats, four young skunks, and a crow named Poe.

The Wish Master, by Betty Ren. Wright Holiday House, 2000.

Take a small, timid boy and put him in an unfamiliar setting where no one has time for him, and you have the story of Corby and his mother, who travel to Wisconsin to care for his ailing grandmother. Grandfather has little use for the timid boy, so Corby is left on his own a good deal of the time. He meets Buck Miller, a boy who loves adventure and who talks Corby into going with him at midnight to visit the Wish Master. The Wish Master is a rough column of rock filled with strange markings, and when Corby makes a wish, things don't go the way he expects. His wish might come true in ways he didn't plan.

More Wisconsin Titles

Bauer, Joan. *Hope Was Here*. Putnam, 2000.

Brink, Carol. *Caddie Woodlawn's Family*. Aladdin, 1990.

Cameron, Ann. *The Secret Life of Amanda K. Woods*. Frances Foser Books, 1998.

Carter, Alden. *Up Country*. Putnam, 1989.

Delton, Judy. *Angel's Mother's Wedding*. Houghton Mifflin, 1987.

Eccles, Mary *By Lizzie*. Dial, 2001.

Enright, Elizabeth. *Thimble Summer*. Harcourt, 1955.

Ernst, Kathleen. *Ghosts of Vicksburg*. White Mane Kids, 2003.

Foster, Rory C. *Dr. Wildlife: The Crusade of a Northwoods Veterinarian*. Watts, 1985.

Hannigan, Katherine. *Ida B. and Her Plans to Maximize Fun, Avoid Disaster, and Possibly Save the World*. Greenwillow, 2004.

Lehne, Judith. *Coyote Girl*. Simon & Schuster, 1995.

Sanchez, Alex. *So Hard to Say*. Simon & Schuster, 2004.

Warner, Gertrude Chandler. *Mystery of the Runaway Ghost*. Whitman, 2004.

Wilder, Laura Ingalls. *Little House on the Prairie*. Harper & Row, 1971.

Wilkes, Maria. *Little Clearing in the Woods*. HarperCollins, 1998.

Wilkes, Maria. *Little House in Brookfield*. HarperCollins, 1996.

Wilkes, Maria. *On Top of Concord Hill*. HarperCollins, 2000.

Wilkins, Celia. *A Litte House of Their Own*. HarperCollins, 2005.

Wright, Betty Ren. *Crandall's Castle*. Holiday House, 2003.

Capital: Cheyenne

Largest City: Cheyenne

Entered the Union: July 10, 1890

Tree: Cottonwood

Flower: Indian paintbrush

Bird: Meadowlark

Rivers: North Platte, Bighorn, Green

Nickname: Equality State

Products: Cattle, coal, oil, uranium

Major Tourist Attractions:
Fort Laramie National Historic Site
Devil's Tower, northeast of Gillette
Yellowstone National Park

Land Area: 97,825 square miles

Population 2006: 501,242

Motto: Equal Rights

Trivia

- Wyoming has more cattle than people.

- Half the land in Wyoming is owned by the federal government.

- In 1825 Nellie Ross became the nation's first female governor.

Wyoming Booktalks

The Haymeadow, by Gary Paulsen. Delacorte, 1992.

Fourteen-year-old John Barron is the spitting image of his great-grandfather, who founded the huge Barron Ranch, which was lost to bad debts. John and his father now work on the ranch. The illness of a ranch hand means that John will spend the summer in the hay meadow looking after 6,000 sheep . . . a job he doesn't feel up to, and he hopes against hope that if he can accomplish it, he will finally please his undemonstrative father. John will be alone, except for two horses, four dogs, and all those sheep.

John's first day alone with the sheep is filled with disasters. A lamb is bitten by a rattlesnake, a skunk sprays John and one of the dogs, another dog has an injured paw, and a bobcat stampedes the sheep. A flash flood in the night turns over the wagon and sweeps away the supplies. John is carried along in the rush of water. The camp is wiped out. In the morning John is able to salvage some clothing, food, and dog food.

John spends the next night fighting off coyotes. By dawn three ewes and two lambs are dead. He uses the horses to bring the wagon upright and is injured in the process. He gets the wagon to higher ground and spends the day cleaning the rifle.

John shoots a coyote and drives the others off. He keeps track of the days by carving notches on a willow stick. Slowly John brings order to the camp and begins to enjoy his aloneness. Through it all he relies on his own resourcefulness, ingenuity, and talents to get through.

My Friend Flicka, by Mary O'Hara. HarperCollins, reissued 2008.

The first time that Ken sees Flicka galloping past him on his family's Wyoming horse ranch, he knows she's the yearling he's been longing for. But Flicka comes from a long line of wild horses, and taming her will take more than Ken could ever have imagined. Here is a tale of love, loyalty, true friendship, family, and following your heart to fight for what is right.

Stone Fox, by John Gardiner. HarperCollins, 1980.

Little Willy was worried. Not just a little bit worried, like when he overslept that one morning and found the chickens had eaten his breakfast, but a lot worried. The worry began the morning grandfather would not get out of bed. Grandfather was usually the first one up and had half the farm chores done before Willy stirred. On the morning grandfather did not get up, Willy was so worried that he ran to get the doctor. She gave grandfather a real thorough examination but could find nothing wrong with him. "Some folks just decide to stop living," she said, "and there is not much anyone can do about it until they change their minds." Willy was determined to get grandfather to change his mind! The potato crop was ready for harvest, and Willy managed it alone by hitching up his dog, Searchlight, to the plow. But when the tax man came Willy didn't know *what* to do. The tax man talked about selling the farm for back taxes. "But we always pay the bills on time," Willy protested. "Not the tax bills," the tax man replied. "You owe ten years' back taxes. That comes to about five hundred dollars." Five hundred dollars! Willy had never seen so much money. Grandfather couldn't help. He just laid in bed and stared at the ceiling. How was Willy going to raise five hundred dollars? He watched the taxman's retreating back. "You can't take our farm!" Willy screamed.

The tax man turned around and smiled through his yellow-stained teeth. "Oh, yes we can," he said.

Red Dog, by Bill Wallace. Simon & Schuster, 2002.

In the rugged Wyoming territory, the red pup is Adam's best friend. Adam and his family live in a lonely cabin in the mountains, facing the dangers of the wilderness. Adam's father must make a week-long trip to Cheyenne, and Adam becomes the man of the family. Everything goes smoothly until three cutthroat gold prospectors come crashing into the cabin and hold the family at gunpoint. Late that night Adam manages to escape. Unfortunately the men let the red pup loose, and the one thing that dog does best is track Adam. Will the pup lead the men to Adam? And if it does, can Adam still save his family?

More Wyoming Titles

Calhoun, B. *Out of Place.* Scientific American, 1994.

Collier, James Lincoln. *Bloody Country.* Four Winds, 1976.

Ehrlich, Gretel. *A Blizzard Year.* Hyperion, 1999.

Henry, Marguerite. *San Domingo: The Medicine Hat Stallion.* Macmillan, 1972.

Lundrie, Amy. *Winnie of the Wild Horses.* Four Winds, 1990.

Naylor, Phyllis Reynolds. *Walker's Crossing.* Atheneum, 1999.

Schaefer, Jack. *Shane.* Houghton Mifflin, 2001.

Yep, Laurence. *The Traitor: Golden Mountain Chronicles, 1885.* HarperCollins, 2003.

Part Two

Reader Response
Activities

NOVEL SUMMARY

Title _____

Author _____

Publisher/Date _____

The setting for this novel is the State of _____

This is a story about _____

who wanted _____

_____

but could not because _____

_____

until _____

_____

_____

Main Characters   Brief Description

_____

_____

_____

This novel (circle one) COULD/COULD NOT not have taken place in any other setting because

_____

_____

_____

_____

_____

_____

Standards: 7, 9, 11, 13

DISTINGUISHING FEATURES

Novel Title _____

State _____

Use the pattern that follows to describe sights and activities that can be found in one particular state. Be sure to include information that will clearly identify the state. Sights should be ones that do not exist in any other state. Activities cited should be ones that cannot be done in any other state. For example, one could only take an elevator to the top of the Empire State Building in the State of New York. One could only visit the tomb of Abraham Lincoln in the State of Illinois.

If I lived in or visited _____ (name the state)

I would see (name four unique sights):

1) _____

2) _____

3) _____

4) _____

And I would (name four activities unique to the state):

1) _____

2) _____

3) _____

4) _____

And after all that sightseeing and activity, I would sit down to a delicious meal of (describe a meal that is typical fare in the state):

_____

_____

_____

Standards: 2, 4, 20, 21

WRITE A STATE SONG

Novel Title _____

State _____

List eight unique sights one would see in this state (two sets of four). Give the date (can be a current date or, if your novel takes place in the past, you can give a date in the past and what sights one would see at that particular time in history).

Tune: This Land Is Your Land

1. In (old/new) (name the state) _____

In (date) _____

I saw _____

And _____

I saw _____

And _____

Sights that everyone should see.

2. In (old/new) (name the state) _____

In (date) _____

I saw _____

And _____

I saw _____

And _____

Sights that everyone should see.

Standards: 2, 4, 12, 21

THINKING ABOUT LANDFORMS

Novel Title _____

State _____

Circle those landforms common to your state.

mountain	isthmus	desert	Summit
Lowland	swamp	plain	pinnacle
bayou	arroyo	canyon	glacier
island	isthmus	estuary	selta
peninsula	oasis	plateau	precipice
valley	wetland		

Choose two or more and write a descriptive riddle about each.

Example:

Lots of vegetation covers my dark body. I creep around twisteed trees and tall weeds. My children ae alligators and snakes. Most people avoid me. I am a _____ (swamp)

_____

_____

_____

_____

_____

_____

Standards: 2, 4, 6, 14, 16, 21

THINKING ABOUT PRODUCTS

Novel Title _____

State _____

WHAT IS IN MY SUITCASE?

List several products from the above state.

_____

_____

_____

_____

What product is the state best known for? _____

List ten facts about the product without naming the product.

1. _____

2. _____

3. _____

4. _____

5. _____

6. _____

7. _____

8. _____

9. _____

10. _____

Ask a classmate to say a number between one and ten. Read the clue for that number. The student can guess or pass. The game continues until the product is guessed or all clues have been read.

The product is _____

Standards: 1, 2, 4, 6, 21

THINKING ABOUT FOOD

Novel Title _____

State _____

Choose one food grown or produced in the state. Research its nutritional qualities. Include your research in writing an ode to that food.

Example:

> I am an orange
>
> From fragrant blossom to fully rounded fruit I am plucked from a tree
>
> My leathery rind hides the delicate flesh beneath
>
> My greatest need is to guard my vitamin C which fights the common cold.
>
> My vitamin A keeps eyesight sharp and keen
>
> My job is to strengthen the human immune system
>
> My former home, the tree, will continue to produce my cousins for 50-80 years
>
> I vacation when 40 percent of me is turned into juice
>
> My greatest desire is to bring joy to a child finding me in a Christina's stocking.
>
> I am an orange

Nancy Polette, _Stop the Copying with Wild and Wacky Research Projects_ (Libraries Unlimited, 2008)

Follow this pattern:

I am _____

I am clothed in _____

My greatest need is _____

My cousins are _____

My job is to _____

_____

Within my layers are _____

_____

I vacation _____

My greatest desire is _____

I am _____

Standards: 1, 2, 4, 6, 21

THINKING ABOUT WILDLIFE

Novel Title _____

State _____

Choose an animal mentioned in the novel or one native to the state. Include as much information as possible about the animal in an Infinitive Poem.

Example:

>All I wanted was
>
>>To swim freely in the clear waters of the Mississippi.
>>
>>To nest in a sheltered place.
>>
>>To grow to a weight of 42 pounds or more
>>
>>To make my home in clear, moving water
>
>But I didn't want
>
>>To swim in a muddy river
>>
>>To feel the sharp hook from a fisherman's line
>>
>>To try to survive in winter in a shallow lake
>>
>>To become someone's catfish dinner
>>
>>To become one of many endangered species.

Animal

>All I wanted was
>>To
>>
>>To
>>
>>To
>>
>>To
>>
>>To
>
>But I didn't want
>>To
>>
>>To
>>
>>To
>>
>>To
>>
>>To

Standards: 2, 4, 6, 14, 16, 21

From *Reading the Fifty States: Booktalks, Response Activities, and More* by Nancy Polette. Westport, CT: Libraries Unlimited. Copyright © 2009.

SAVING THE STATE

Novel Title _____

State _____

Land forms (mountains, plains, rivers, lakes) are often important to the economy of a state. For example, Colorado welcomes many tourists each winter who come to ski in the mountains. The fishing industry is very important to the State of Washington. If rivers, lakes, and streams are polluted and natural resources are depleted, everyone suffers.

Begin a crusade to protect the resources of your state. Create a NEWSPAPER CUTTING REPORT. Gather and display at least ten of the following items found in your daily paper:

1. An article about a natural resource that is not wildlife.

2. A picture or article about an endangered animal.

3. A major water source.

4. Something that needs to be conserved.

5. A product good for the environment.

6. Good advice for saving something.

7. Someone to write about an environmental problem.

8. A picture or article about recycling.

9. An energy producer that pollutes.

10. Something that poisons the air we breathe.

11. A safe way to dispose of trash.

12. An article about or picture of a landfill.

Standards: 1, 3, 4, 5, 11, 19

From _Reading the Fifty States: Booktalks, Response Activities, and More_ by Nancy Polette. Westport, CT: Libraries Unlimited. Copyright © 2009.

CITY BINGO

Novel Title _____

State _____

Create Bingo Boards with the names of sixteen cities in your state.

List one fact for each city. The caller reads a fact, and players who know the answer can cover that city on their boards. The first player to get four across or down is the winner.

FACT CITY

1. _____
2. _____
3. _____
4. _____
5. _____
6. _____
7. _____
8. _____
9. _____
10. _____
11. _____
12. _____
13. _____
14. _____
15. _____
16. _____

Standards: 3, 10, 17, 20

SIGHTS AND SOUNDS

Novel Title _____

State _____

I am ST CHARLES in 2008

I am the sound of

Clippity clop horses pulling carriages

Instruments tuning up on the bandstand

Slap whap of passing river barges

The chatter of 1,200 citizens

Spitting of coals on barbeque grills

The mournful whistle of the Norfolk & Western

Swish, swish of brooms as antique shops open for business.

My colors are

The oozing brown of the muddy Missouri

The dull red of much-traveled cobblestone streets

The bright red caboose that beckons crowds to the riverfront

The red, white, and blue banners decorating the bandstand.

The silver star of law and order worn by the sheriff

The pink cheeks of excited children watching the night sky lit with fireworks.

I am St. Charles, Missouri on July 4.

I am _____ in _____

I am the sound of

My colors are

I am _____ in _____

Standards: 2, 4, 6, 14, 16, 21

FAMOUS CITIZENS

Novel Title _____

State _____

Choose a famous citizen from your state and complete the bio poem.

Name _____

I am _____

I wonder _____

_____

I hear _____

_____

I see _____

_____

I want _____

_____

I pretend _____

_____

I touch _____

_____

I cry _____

_____

I say _____

_____

I try _____

_____

I give _____

_____

I am (Name) _____

Source of Information _____

_____

Standards: 2, 4, 6, 14, 16, 21

From *Reading the Fifty States: Booktalks, Response Activities, and More*
by Nancy Polette. Westport, CT: Libraries Unlimited. Copyright © 2009.

THE FAMOUS AND THE INFAMOUS

Novel Title _____

State _____

Famous people generally are considered to have made _positive_ contributions to society.

Infamous people generally have made _negative_ contributions to society.

Read about famous and infamous people from your state. List two famous and two infamous people from the state.

_____

_____

_____

_____

Which of the two people you listed do you consider to be the most infamous?

_____

Why? _____

_____

If any famous or infamous person from real life was mentioned in the novel you read, list the name here. Tell why the person was famous or infamous.

_____

_____

Rating Scale 1 = least valuable 2 = most valuable	Affects Many People	Easy Access	Long Lasting Effect	Your Criteria

If the person whose contribution you chose as most valuable had lived or done his or her work in another state, or had been born in another state, what would be missing from the state noted above today? _____

Standards: 1, 2, 4, 5, 19

THAT'S GOOD, THAT'S BAD REPORT

Novel Title _____

State _____

Choose a famous citizen from your state. Use the pattern below to write about that person's life.

Name: Marian Anderson **State:** Pennsylvania

Marian Anderson was born in Philadelphia, Pennsylvania on February 27, 1897. It was obvious from an early age that she had a beautiful voice.

That's good!

No, that's bad because her poor family could not afford musical training for her.

That's bad.

No, it was good because she kept on singing and won a scholarship to study abroad, then returned to the United States to give concerts.

That's good

No, it was bad because she was denied the opportunity to give a concert in Constitution Hall because of her color.

That's bad.

Not really, because 75,000 people came to hear her sing at the Lincoln Memorial.

Name _____

(fill in first statement about the person) _____

_____

That's good.

No, it was bad because _____

_____

That' s bad.

No, it was good because _____

_____

That' s good.

Not really because _____

_____

That's bad.

Not entirely, because _____

_____

That's good.

Yes, it is because _____

_____

Standards: 2, 4, 6, 14, 16, 21

From _Reading the Fifty States: Booktalks, Response Activities, and More_ by Nancy Polette. Westport, CT: Libraries Unlimited. Copyright © 2009.

BIOGRAPHY LIMERICKS

Novel Title _____

State _____

Many historical incidents have been told as narrative poems. *The Charge of the Light Brigade* and *The Midnight Ride of Paul Revere* are well-known narrative poems that are based on actual incidents in history. Here is a limerick about the Missouri outlaw, Jesse James.

JESSE JAMES

A bandit he was sure enough
So daring, so bold and so tough
He said, "Give me your money,
I'm not being funny
My boys and I always play rough."
No matter if sunshine or rain
Jesse got gold by robbing a train
He was not very brave
Hid out in a cave
Where he hid all his ill-gotten gain.
Now Jesse rarely was bored
Spent hours counting his hoard
Then while up on a chair
Bullets flew through the air
He was shot by a coward named Ford.

Select a famous person from your novel's state. Research facts about the person by using the encyclopedia and books on the subject found in the library. Write and illustrate a narrative poem based on the facts you find.

Title: _____

_____

_____

_____

_____

_____

_____

Standards: 2, 4, 6, 14, 16, 21

From *Reading the Fifty States: Booktalks, Response Activities, and More* by Nancy Polette. Westport, CT: Libraries Unlimited. Copyright © 2009.

GENERALITIES AND STEREOTYPES

Novel Title _____

State _____

Sometimes people generalize about a particular region or state. Have you heard these generalizations?

      All people in Florida have suntans.

      Everything in Texas is big!

      People in Missouri have to be shown a thing before they will believe it.

1.   What is the most generally accepted statement about your state?

    _____

    _____

2.   What evidence, if any, did you find to support this statement in the novel you read?

    _____

    _____

3.   Now look at your local newspapers and cut out pictures about people in this state that prove that this is not always true. Attach the pictures to this page and be prepared to defend your choices.

4.   Was any character in the novel you read a stereotype of a person from this state? If so, in what way?

    _____

    _____

    _____

    _____

    _____

Standards: 2, 4, 8, 10, 11, 15

WRITE A FACT OR FICTION BOOK

Novel Title _____

State _____

1.   Gather interesting facts about the state.

2.   Group your facts.

   Facts about people

   Facts about places

   Facts about products

   Facts about geographical features

   Facts about historical events

   Other facts

3.   Choose the most interesting facts to use in your book.

4.   State a fact on one page.

5.   Tell on the next page whether it is fact or fiction, and why.

6.   Change some of the facts so that your can explain why the statement is not true.

FACT OR FICTION?: Alaska was the last of the fifty states to be admitted to the Union.

FICTION: Alaska was admitted to the Union January 3, 1959. Hawaii was admitted to the Union August 21, 1959, making it the last state to be admitted.

Standards: 2, 4, 6, 14, 16, 21

From *Reading the Fifty States: Booktalks, Response Activities, and More* by Nancy Polette. Westport, CT: Libraries Unlimited. Copyright © 2009.

DESCRIBING BY COMPARING

Novel Title _____

State _____

Try to describe this state by using similes.

Name of the state: _____

List adjectives that describe the state.

_____ _____ _____

_____ _____ _____

Now use these words to write five descriptive sentences about your state. Each sentence must contain a simile; a comparison using the words _like_ or _as_.

EXAMPLE:

The Mississippi River winds along one edge of Missouri like a ribbon at the edge of a valentine. Part of the State of Missouri is shaped like a boot heel.

This device, the simile, helps the reader develop much better mental images about the state you are describing. Write your similes below.

1. _____

_____

2. _____

_____

3. _____

_____

4. _____

_____

5. _____

_____

Standards: 1, 2, 4, 15, 16

RUNNING FOR OFFICE

Novel Title _____

State _____

    In a *democracy* people decide together what laws are necessary for the good of all the citizens. To make this possible, the people of a state elect representatives to gather together at the state capital to pass laws and make decisions that will affect all citizens. Most states have *state representatives* and *state senators* who determine what the laws will be.

List the qualities you feel a *state representative* should have to do a good job of passing laws that affect all the people.

_____

_____

_____

Look at your list. Which of the qualities listed does the main character have in the novel you read?

Character's name _____

Qualities _____

_____

_____

Give at least two reasons why you feel this character would make a good *state representative*.

_____

_____

_____

_____

Standards: 2, 4, 5, 8, 19

From *Reading the Fifty States: Booktalks, Response Activities, and More* by Nancy Polette. Westport, CT: Libraries Unlimited. Copyright © 2009.

FAMOUS FIRSTS!

Novel Title _____

State _____

    Here is a famous first any state would want to claim!

       The first ice cream cone was made in St Louis, Missouri.

    The reference book, _Famous First Facts_ is filled with first things that happened in every state in the United States.

Find your state in _Famous First Facts_. List a famous first fact for your state in each of these areas:

People _____

_____

Inventions _____

_____

Places _____

_____

Foods _____

_____

Your choice _____

_____

Standards: 4, 10, 11, 14, 19

RESEARCH REPORT: THE A–Z REPORT

Novel Title _____

State _____

Name of the state _____

Use 26 phrases or sentences A–Z to tell about your state.

A _____

B _____

C _____

D _____

E _____

F _____

G _____

H _____

I _____

J _____

K _____

L _____

M _____

N _____

O _____

P _____

Q _____

R _____

S _____

T _____

U _____

V _____

W _____

X _____

Y _____

Z _____

Standards: 2, 4, 5, 8, 15

Index

About the Author

NANCY POLETTE is an educator with over 30 years' experience. She has authored more than 150 professional books. She lives and works in Missouri, where she is a professor at Lindenwood University.